LADY HODGSON

Frontispiece

THE
SIEGE OF KUMASSI

BY

LADY HODGSON
WIFE OF SIR FREDERIC HODGSON, K.C.M.G.
LATE GOVERNOR OF THE GOLD COAST

WITH MANY ILLUSTRATIONS
A MAP AND A PLAN

London
C. Arthur Pearson Ltd.
Henrietta Street
1901

PLYMOUTH
WILLIAM BRENDON AND SON
PRINTERS

PREFACE

IN writing an account of the siege of Kumassi, in which my husband and I found ourselves involved very shortly after our arrival there, and of the events which immediately preceded and followed it, and in which I had a share, I have been actuated by a desire to place on record, while the facts are clearly in my mind, an experience which may be of value to those who keep themselves in touch with events of interest in outlying portions of our empire. It has been my aim to state everything as I saw it, without embellishment, and while it is possible that some may think that here and there I have expressed opinions which are too candid, I can only say that they are opinions which I hold.

I have thought that a slight sketch of the social life of the Gold Coast would also be acceptable, drawn from a woman's point of view, and although

9

Preface

it is in some degree outside our subject, I have ventured to include it, adding also a few words from experience upon the gold prospects.

For many of the photographs I am under a debt of gratitude to Mr. P. A. McCann, of the Liverpool Ashanti Gold Concessions. My own photographs, and I had taken several during the siege the reproduction of which would have been very interesting, were lost with all my other effects during the early part of our march out of Kumassi.

CHYLTON DENE, SURBITON,
January, 1901.

CONTENTS

Contents

LIST OF ILLUSTRATIONS

List of Illustrations

THE SIEGE OF KUMASSI

CHAPTER I

A PLUNGE INTO PERIL

NOT many days after my arrival at Accra in November, 1899, I learnt with some little dismay that my husband was making arrangements to visit Ashanti, and that I was included in them. It is the rule for a governor to visit his outlying provinces as often as possible, and the time had come when another tour of inspection in that part of the Protectorate was desirable. It was to be taken in the ordinary course of affairs, and there was not any suspicion of trouble ahead, for there had been no reports indicating that the people were either discontented or disloyal. Had this been the case he would never have thought of taking me with him, nor would he have left Accra without making provision for any emergency that might arise. We started on our journey with no prospect of trouble beyond the discomforts of bush travelling, and I confess that I was feeling not a little proud of the fact that I should be the first Englishwoman to enter Kumassi.

Great were the preparations for our departure in March, and, terrible to relate, the date fixed for it was the 13th of the month! We were nearly prevented from starting on this date of ill-omen to the superstitious by a serious case of illness which our doctor had in charge. Everything in West Africa gives way to health, and one's best emotions are forthcoming when a friend is laid on a bed of fever. So it happened that on the 12th it was almost decided not to start until the doctor was willing to leave his patient; but this disarrangement of plans made so many complications that in the end it was decided to start on the 13th, only putting off the hour from 8 a.m. until 2 p.m., in the hope that the doctor would be able to leave with us instead of having to overtake us—as indeed he did, for the patient took a turn for the better.

It had taken days to pack the stores and wines that we were to carry with us. The "chop boxes" had been packed so as to weigh not more than the regulation 56 lbs. "Chop" is the term used in West Africa for provisions. A common expression

A Plunge into Peril

among those who care to use West African slang or pidgin-English is "pass chop," which means "bring in dinner," or "give me my breakfast." It is astonishing what a little makes up 56 lbs. when put into a chop box, and it is with dismay that you see the rapidity with which the number of boxes multiplies; but the fact is that the box itself is heavy, having to be made strong and solid in order to stand the hard wear and tear incidental to bush travelling.

When you start on an expedition up country it means taking everything with you, from matches upwards; household furniture in the form of travelling tables and chairs, beds, baths, crockery, all cooking utensils—in fact everything in a compressed form, and woe betide the traveller if anything is forgotten. The natives who have been selected as carriers arrive in charge of their headman some two hours before the time fixed for the start, and are lined up in a row. When the roll has been called, and a last inspection made of them, they are brought one by one to the loads, and each man, taking the load allotted to him, returns to his place, and puts it down in front of him. When once a man has obtained his load, it is his until the end of the journey.

A Plunge into Peril

It is marvellous how each carrier can always tell his load among a number that are all so much alike; many of them twist into the padlock of the box a piece of coloured rag or a twig, or put upon the box a small mark, known only to themselves; they can tell in a moment when they resume their loads if anything has been added to the contents, and grumbling often ensues, for although the addition has not made the load appreciably heavier, it has perhaps spoilt the balance, and made it not quite so comfortable on the head as before. No complaints, however, are heard if the load has been lightened since it was last parted with. Each carrier ties on to the top of his load his worldly possessions for the journey, consisting generally of a native mat to sleep on, and a small bundle of rags—I cannot call them clothes, for the costumes are varied and vague; also a shallow native cooking-pot, in which he cooks his food, and from which he eats it.

After saying good-bye to the officials who had come to see us off, we were escorted from Government House to the outskirts of the town by a guard of honour of volunteers, with the drum and fife band of the corps. There was also a crowd of natives, some honouring us by swelling the crowd, and some gathered to see their friends and relatives start upon their long journey.

There is always, I think, a keen pleasure in seeking the unknown, and we started for Kumassi looking forward to our trip with excitement, never dreaming of what sufferings were to be ours, nor even thinking of the fatigue and discomforts of the twelve days' journey before us. The mode of travelling on the Gold Coast is in hammocks, and a tedious, irritating mode it is, for the hammock is unrestful, and at the end of a day's journey you are stiff and cramped. There are two kinds : one is the ordinary hammock, in which the occupant travels lying down, and the other is known as a sitting hammock. The latter is by far the more comfortable, and it certainly is not so hot ; it has also the advantage of allowing the occupant to see where he is going. The angle of the sitting hammock can be changed by means of a foot-rest, and this is a great relief to your tired body on a long day's journey.

To every hammock are allowed eight men, four carrying you when the road is wide enough for two to be abreast, and four ready to relieve their comrades on duty, or to assist them with the hammock over difficult ground. The hammock

A Plunge into Peril

is made of stout canvas roped on to a bamboo pole, at each end of which is a flat cross-piece of wood which rests upon the bearers' heads, as two men walk in front and two behind. They swing you along at a fair pace, four miles an hour being considered good going. Sometimes they take it into their heads to run with you, and this is far from agreeable, for the shaking and swinging of the hammock is most unpleasant.

Hammock bearers are a merry set of men as a rule, and will keep the conversation going with much hilarity amongst themselves. You often wish you could join in, and so pass an hour or two of the time that hangs so heavily in bush travelling ; but their language is quite unintelligible, and you feel somewhat annoyed that they cannot even understand enough English to obey your orders. For instance, you may call out to them to stop from running, and they will run all the faster, thinking you are enjoying the fun—as they are—of outstripping other hammocks of the party ; instead of which you are getting a shaking that seems to make every bone in your body rattle. If any European lady is thinking of travelling in this fashion up country in West Africa, let her be wise in time, and take my advice, which is similar to that given by *Punch* "to people about to marry"—"Don't!"

The thought of ladies travelling in the interior reminds me of a Belgian lady, who came out to the Gold Coast by the steamer on which I too was travelling to Accra. Her husband was going out to prospect for gold, and to obtain concessions of auriferous land from native chiefs. Very foolishly he was taking his wife with him, for he was completely ignorant of the country of his quest. She hardly spoke English at all, and he not too well. In conversation I learnt that they were uncertain whether a railway ran to the part they wished to reach; but anyhow, failing this means of conveyance, they had arranged for a caravan to be in waiting for them on their arrival at Cape Coast. I tried gently to combat their preconceived ideas, and to explain that hammocks would be the only possible way of travelling to their destination. I had not then had much experience myself of bush life, or of hammock travelling, but I knew enough to feel certain that the life they were about to embark on was not fitted for a woman, and I wish now that I had been even more emphatic than I was in my warning to the man not to take his wife with him into the interior. She had been during the voyage very bright and lively, but when the time came for her to go ashore at Cape Coast she must needs put on one of her best frocks, and she manifested deep distress and became much annoyed when advised to change it—it was a pretty blue and black silk—for a more suitable one for the surf to disport itself upon. I suppose she thought there would be an admiring crowd on the beach.

I took so much interest in her that I was constantly asking officers on their return to headquarters if they had met this lady up-country. At last one day I heard news of her. An officer had passed through the place where they were staying, and had dined with them. They were living in a native hut, and no other white people were near them; she was looking ill and worn, and he, poor man, had not found the Eldorado he came out to seek. They had made a little garden round the hut, in which they were growing vegetables and English flowers. A few weeks later I heard of them again. The husband had been very ill, and was then at Cape Coast out of his mind. She had brought him down in this pitiful state quite alone, except for her native servants. So all their bright hopes had fled in the short space of less than four months. Of course this is an exceptional

A Plunge into Peril

case, and about the only one I have known of a lady going gold prospecting with her husband in West Africa, but it may serve as a warning.

West Africa in its most civilised aspect is not a kind place to the European woman; if ever she has had even a pretence to good looks, the climate demands them, and takes them from her if she stays too long under its influence. There is also a terrible battle to be fought against the climate in its attempt to rob you of your memory. After a few months' residence in West Africa it becomes most difficult to remember small events, and a constant effort has to be made to prevent things from slipping from your mind.

On arriving at the village where the first night was to be passed, we found the tent already pitched and the people all on the look-out for our arrival. It was a very small and dirty village, and crowded with natives, but perhaps our own large party gave it this crowded appearance, for we numbered some two hundred and fifty, including the Hausa soldier escort of thirty men. We were not quite pleased with the spot on which our tent had been pitched, and wandered about trying to find a better site for it further away from so many native huts. As we walked down the principal street of the village we came upon a stream where the people were washing clothes and bathing. Evening is always the time chosen by the native for his tub. We thought the other side of this stream looked more inviting, and made the men know that we wished to cross over. There was a very leaky and rickety canoe into which we were invited to get. This was pushed across the shallow stream by two men, while a third stood behind me to steady me, for I was standing, seats being unknown in a native canoe. We found that distance had lent enchantment to the surroundings, and that the land was not only swampy, but otherwise entirely unfitted for our camp, and we had to content ourselves with the site already selected.

My next visit was to my cook to see where his kitchen was, and when I found him, the sight was one which made it best to shut my eyes if I wished to enjoy, or even eat, any dinner. He had been allotted a portion of a very dirty hut in a still more dirty compound. The native cook is a very clever man on the march, and will give you as tasty a dinner as if he had prepared it in his own kitchen with everything to hand: this is always supposing that he has proper materials, and is not tied down to the warming of tinned meats or fish, which is more often than not what an ordinary bush traveller

SIR FREDERIC M. HODGSON

Face page 24

A Plunge into Peril

has to put up with. The natives have a very simple arrangement for a stove, namely, three large round stones made of burnt earth, in the centre of which the fire is lighted, while the pots are balanced on the stones. For baking, the native uses an oven of burnt earth very similar in character to the Dutch oven used in England. Most of the cooking is done in the open, but the native appears to have no fear of burning his hut down, as, when occasion requires it, he, or perhaps more properly speaking she—for the family cooking arrangements fall to the lot of the women of the establishment—makes the fire inside the hut, or just by the door, so that the flames and smoke blacken the walls. As a general rule the hut is built of dried earth, the roofing being of thatch, made of coarse dried grass, which is very inflammable; yet, strange to say, very few fires occur.

This night was the first time I had slept in a tent, and I cannot say that I enjoyed it. I found myself many a time sighing for the comforts of my bedroom, and wishing that I had not embarked upon the journey to Kumassi. But it is a great thing to go through life cheerfully, and as I was embarked on a congenial expedition, having always wished to see Kumassi, I had no intention

A Plunge into Peril

of allowing a few mischances or discomforts to discourage me. Misadventures in a tent while travelling in the bush are many. More than once, for example, a clumsy boy upset my bath all over the floor, and then, with a childlike disregard of the inconvenience caused, aggravatingly enjoyed the fun. I had generally to undertake some part of my dressing in the morning outside the tent, and had there an admiring crowd of critics round me. My long hair was a great attraction, and the brushing of it was a source of amusement and wonder.

Our party consisted of the Governor and myself, the Private Secretary, Dr. Chalmers, and the Acting Director of Public Works. We generally managed to be on the move every morning at seven o'clock, and to keep on our journey until eleven, when a halt was made for about two hours for tiffin and rest. Our travelling tables and deck chairs formed the load of a good-natured, jovial little carrier who trudged merrily along with us, and was always at hand when they were wanted. The meal carried ready-cooked did not take long to set before our hungry party, and travelling gives one a wonderful appetite! Often the days were very hot and fatiguing, and I must confess

that when the novelty of bush travelling wore
off I found it rather tedious work, for every day
was very much the same, and the scenery for
the most part monotonous.

The forest is cool and shady, and gigantic trees
tower overhead, making you feel a very small
being indeed amid such grandeur. There were
some beautiful bits of scenery here and there, and
at times we came upon groves of palms, or it
might be of bamboos, forming enormous arches
delightful to pass under, so quaint were they and
weird. Not many flowers were met with. They
seemed to have been crushed out of existence
by the wild exuberance of the forest trees, which
with the wealth of undergrowth monopolised all
the available space; but occasionally I saw some
magnificent white lilies and varieties of convolvulus,
and here and there a tree, bearing large and
gorgeous red flowers somewhat resembling a tulip,
gave out a blaze of colour which lit up brightly
the prevailing green, so that the sudden contrast
charmed the eye.

We spent one night at the Basel Mission House
at Nsaba, and were entertained with great hospi-
tality by the missionaries who were stationed there.
Nsaba is a very large native town, and the mission

A Plunge into Peril

station is a typical one, placed on rising ground
on the immediate outskirts of the town. This
rising ground had been entirely cleared of undergrowth, and with few exceptions all the trees had
been cut down. The dwelling, like all the houses
of Basel missionaries, was substantially built of
wood, with a shingled roof, and the rooms were
large and spacious. The ground floor was given
up to schoolrooms, for with all the missionary
bodies in the Gold Coast education goes hand-in-
hand with religion, and above, on the first floor,
were the bed- and sitting-rooms of the missionaries,
surrounded by a broad and roofed veranda, the
floor of which afforded shade to the rooms below.
Close to the house was the Lutheran church, built
for the mission by the natives; and in front was
a large cleared area of some six acres, in which
the elder boys under instruction in the school were
taught agriculture—chiefly the cultivation of cocoa
and coffee, products for which the soil seemed
admirably adapted.

I met the Commissioner of the Winneba district
at Nsaba, which is almost in the centre of his
district. He had come there to see the Governor,
who had summoned him for the purpose of select-
ing a site for the erection of a small cottage

A Plunge into Peril

bungalow, as it was the Governor's wish that all commissioners should periodically leave their stations on the coast, and by travelling, and at times residing in some central town in their districts, should make themselves acquainted with the native kings and chiefs, ascertain the wants and requirements of the people, look into the due administration of justice in the native courts, see that the native roads are kept cleared and fit for traffic, interest the people in agriculture, and in every possible way push trade and commercial enterprise. There was also a dispute about the occupation of the stool of Nsaba which the Governor desired to settle, and for which purpose we remained a day at the mission station. Some three years earlier the head chief of the district— Nsaba being the place of residence—had been removed by the people for intemperate habits and gross oppression, and his nephew had been selected as ruler in his stead. The choice had not proved satisfactory. The new chief showed himself to be weak and easily led, and had fallen into unnecessary litigation, with the result that the legal expenses were so heavy that he had to place himself in the hands of the ever-ready usurer. He had in consequence mortgaged the revenues of the stool, which was being demanded as security for the debt. The sub-chiefs of the district, filled with resentment, had deposed him from the stool, which they refused to part with to the usurer, and the district was once more without a ruler. This was the previous chief's opportunity, for he was now intriguing to recover his lost power, and the people, many of whom favoured him, were fast breaking up into parties, so that conflicts between the various factions were imminent.

A large meeting was held in the town, at which all the sub-chiefs and interested parties were present. The whole situation was disclosed with customary detail, and the Governor, having listened attentively to the various statements, gave his decision that neither the old nor the recent ruler was to be restored to the stool, but that a fresh selection altogether must be made, and his name submitted to the Commissioner for approval, when, if approved, the election was to proceed in accordance with native custom; further, that the stool was not to be given up as a pledge for the debt, and that the debt was one which the Government would examine, and, after reducing it to equitable proportions, would recommend the people to get rid of by early payment. The decision was received with much favour, and the sub-chiefs departed to their respective villages, after the usual ceremony of hand-shaking, to discuss their interview with the Governor.

It was with much reluctance that I left this hospitable station, and plunged once more into the forest, and life in a tent. The people of the villages through which we passed always gave us a hearty welcome, and in the villages at which we stayed the night the chiefs and all the people turned out to pay their respects to the Governor, and received him according to native etiquette with much drum-beating and dancing. The offering of gifts is a time-honoured native custom, and as soon as we reached our tent a long line of people would appear bearing presents from the chief, such as yams, eggs, fruit, and, if he was a wealthy personage, perhaps a sheep or some fowls. Then humbler folk would bring their offerings, which were similar, but only in smaller quantities. A suitable return has to be made in every case, a gift of money, usually somewhat beyond the value of the presentation, being the general method of discharging the obligation, and showing appreciation of the articles presented. Much offence is caused if this return is made at once. According to native custom the donor must retire, and shortly afterwards be sent for to receive it. When the donors are many this becomes a lengthy and tedious business.

Native children are not very attractive—they are generally dirty and without clothes; still, it was amusing to watch their antics, and their delight at the novel sight of a governor and his party staying in their village, doing things quite strange and comical in their sight, such as sitting at table, eating out of plates, and using knives and forks. They would stand, fortunately at some little distance, and stare with all their might and main, making from time to time comments among themselves when anything appeared to them unusually droll.

We were eight days travelling to Prahsu, where there is a fairly good Government rest-house, and here, as the Governor had received mails, we stayed for a day and a half. Prahsu is not by any means in itself a delectable place. It is practically a Government post, where, since the Ashanti War of 1872–3, a detachment of Hausas has been kept, and where also a telegraph station has been established. It is of importance, as being the point on the main road from Cape Coast to Kumassi, where travellers cross from the Colony into Ashanti and back by means of the ferry service

A Plunge into Peril

which is maintained by the Government, the river Prah being here the boundary between the Colony and Ashanti.

The river scenery is very pretty, and had it not been for the heavy air, the humming of hundreds of insects, and the buzzing of what is known as the six o'clock beetle, it might have been possible to delude oneself into thinking that we were back in England and gazing out upon the banks of the Thames. Here it was that the services of the Acting Director of Public Works came into play, for the Governor wished to throw a bridge across the river in order to facilitate the large traffic on the road, and wanted levels taken and a site for the work selected. Already the construction by the Government of an excellent road between Cape Coast and Prahsu was nearing completion. We had not travelled by it, but had come from Accra by a somewhat difficult and less-frequented road, as the Governor wished to leave the beaten track for our return journey, having work to do at Nsaba and other of the places through which we had travelled. At Prahsu the river rises and falls with great rapidity, and when in flood is very swift. At times it overflows its banks, and then indeed Prahsu must be a very undesirable place of residence.

CHAPTER II

DENSE FOREST AND SHEER HILLS

IT is strange how the scenery changes when the river is crossed and the traveller finds himself in Ashanti-land. The forest becomes grander, and sterner in its grandeur, and the road, leading over undulating ground, is more picturesque and pleasant. We had so far been very fortunate in having had no rain, and we hoped to reach Kumassi and to return before the rains began in earnest, for we knew by repute that the road to the north of the Prah was by no means good, and led over many swamps and streams. It is a four days' ordinary journey between Prahsu and Kumassi, and at each halting-place—namely at Fumsu, Kwisa, and Esumeja—comfortable rest-houses have recently been built by the Government for the accommodation of Government officers and others who have to pass up and down the road. These rest-houses are available on certain conditions, and by a small money payment, to Europeans prospecting for gold,

and are most comfortable, being not only in every way far superior to the average native hut, but also placed on sanitary sites. I hailed them with delight, for I had become very tired of tent life, and was glad to have a roof over my head once more.

Fumsu and Kwisa are in Adansi, and Esumeja is in Bekwai. Between the Adansis and Bekwais there has long been a feud. The former, under the provisions of the treaty made by Sir Garnet Wolseley with the Ashantis, and signed at Fomena on the 13th February, 1874, were disengaged from the Ashanti confederation and made independent of it, their country being made a buffer country between Ashanti and the Colony. Swelling with pride at their new and important position, the Adansis, thinking that they would have the support of a British force, and in spite of warnings and assurances to the contrary, declared war against their powerful neighbours the Bekwais, and at once paid the penalty for their temerity. The whole tribe was driven across the Prah, and the King and majority of the people begged permission to be allowed to locate themselves at Nsaba, through which place we had recently passed. The Bekwais, by right of conquest and in accordance with native custom, annexed a large portion of the Adansi country—that portion, in fact, which they knew to be auriferous, and a large part of which now lies within the concession of the Ashanti Goldfields Corporation. When, after the bloodless expedition of 1896 under General Sir Francis Scott, the Adansis left the Colony and returned to their tribal lands, they found themselves shorn of the part in question and of the wealth which they, quite as well as their conquerors, knew that it contained, and they found also that the Government was not disposed to range itself against native custom, and to secure for them the return of the coveted strip. It appears to me to be important to note this situation of affairs in the light of recent events, as in some measure it accounts for the Bekwais and Adansis taking opposite sides, and the latter throwing in their lot against the Government.

Close to the Government rest-house at Fumsu runs the stream of that name, and a few miles further on are the steep Moinsi Hills, on the other side of which lies the village of Kwisa. At the foot of these hills is the village of Brafu Edru, where there is a Government telegraph station, and where we halted for rest and tiffin before undertaking the ascent. The road up the hills

Dense Forest and Sheer Hills

could be plainly seen, for no attempt had been made to ease the journey by a devious track. It just went straight up, without regard to obstacles, as if climbing was the easiest thing in the world. My hammock-men were very good, and determined to show me they were strong men, for up this almost impassable path they carried me, and only once had I to get out and walk at a particularly difficult place. After a rough and trying journey we reached Kwisa shortly before four o'clock in the afternoon. From the top of the Moinsi Hills we had a splendid view of the landscape stretching out on all sides towards Kumassi. Always and everywhere the same impenetrable forest, the monotony being only relieved by the different shades of green, with here and there in the near distance a splash of red colouring, marking where the red tulip tree had managed to assert itself and relieve the universal sameness.

At Kwisa were assembled the King of Adansi, his court party, and several of his chiefs, and the Governor arranged to receive them at five o'clock. Long before that hour the King had taken up his place on the ground where the meeting was to be held, and surrounded by his chiefs and principal officials he waited in state for the Governor's arrival. Shortly before five o'clock one of the King's linguists came to the rest-house to say that the King sent his compliments to the Governor and hoped that His Excellency would not long delay his arrival, as he had been waiting for some time. I remember my husband's astonishment at receiving this unusual message, and his remarking to me that the King appeared not to know his position towards the Governor; but he returned the answer that the meeting had been arranged for five o'clock, and that the King might reckon upon his attending it punctually, which would be in a few minutes. At five o'clock the Governor, dressed in his uniform of major commanding the Gold Coast Volunteers, arrived at the appointed place, was received by a guard of honour of the Hausas, and took his seat in front of the King, the other European officers sitting on his right and left.

After the usual interchange of compliments, during which the Governor expressed his pleasure at meeting the King in his own country, the King presented a letter which was handed to him by one of his linguists. The King is a very old man, and blind, and appeared to be the object of the greatest care and solicitude on the part of his officials, who endeavoured to anticipate his every want. The letter, which had been written by the King's secretary,—a semi-educated scholar from the Coast—expressed in general terms the pleasure of the King and his people at receiving a visit from the Governor of the Gold Coast. Then was handed to the Governor a second letter, in which the King set forth a list of grievances from which he and his people considered themselves to be suffering. I was watching the meeting within ear-shot from the fence around the compound of the rest-house.

Among the grievances was that against the Bekwais for annexing some of the gold-bearing land of the tribe, and a complaint that the Bekwais received from the Ashanti Goldfields Corporation twice as large an annual payment in respect of their concession as they themselves received. I remember the look of astonishment on the faces of the King's chiefs and linguists when, referring to this matter, the Governor reminded the King that he, when in exile at Nsaba, had sent one of his linguists to Accra in 1889, to ask the question whether when his tribe returned to Adansi the land in question would belong to him or to the King of Bekwai, and had been told that the occupation of the land by the latter was in accordance with native custom, and would not be disturbed. "And," added the Governor, pointing to one of the linguists, "that is the linguist who brought the question and to whom the reply was given." "*Mpāre*" ("it is true"), was the exclamation of those present. The King had evidently hoped that a lapse of over ten years would have obliterated the recollection of the visit, and of the decision then given. It was another instance of the dogged persistence of the native in matters affecting his welfare. Of the other grievances, some only referred to matters which the Governor had come to Ashanti to look into, others were exaggerated, and one was without any sort of foundation—at least, so I gathered from what was said. At the close of the meeting the King presented a gift of sheep and eggs, and received afterwards a return present in the shape of money. When the Governor came back I met him and told him I had watched the proceedings. His remark to me was, "Well, I don't like the demeanour of the King and his officials; there seemed to be a tendency to truculence, and I believe the old man means to give trouble in some way or other. I shall have to ascertain what is known against him at Kumassi. However, let us have dinner now and as soon as possible, for the palaver has made me hungry."

Next morning we left Kwisa early, and at Fomena the King and his officials met us to bid us good-bye, and to say that they were starting that afternoon for Kumassi in order to attend the big durbar to which all the Ashanti kings had been summoned.

Throughout our journey from Prahsu we passed many traders carrying rubber and other produce to the coast. Many had come from great distances, and very varied were the types of native met with. The loads were as a rule heavy — much heavier, in fact, than those carried by paid carriers, who decline to carry more than about 60 lbs., but if carrying for themselves their loads will sometimes reach to 100 lbs., and even more.

The barbarous custom of tattooing was everywhere prevalent. We passed many women and men with large designs upon their chests and back; colour did not appear in the tattoo, but in most cases the skin in some way or other had been raised. One of the designs which attracted my attention was an elaborate one of native huts; but figures, birds, and a lattice-work pattern seemed the favourite subjects. To raise the skin thus

must have caused hours of agony and discomfort.
The hairdressing among the women was also very
quaint in many cases. Women are as frequently
seen carrying loads as men; and then, poor things,
they generally have to walk with a baby strapped
on to their backs as an addition to the load on
their heads, and on reaching their destination for
the night hey cannot plead fatigue, but have to
prepare food for the men of their party. The
villages through which we passed were most hospitable to our carriers and the Hausa escort, large
bowls of cooked food and jars of water being
placed conveniently for the men to help themselves
as they passed by, while the owners of these free
gifts sat by and invited them to do so.

We often had palm wine brought to us, and it
would have given great offence if it had not been
accepted and tasted. Palm wine is the native
drink in the forest belt, and if allowed to ferment
it becomes intoxicating. The extraction of this
wine from the tree requires some skill and trouble.
In the first place the selected tree has to be felled;
a fire is then lighted under the trunk, in which an
incision half-way up the stem has been made.
From this incision the sap drops into a large
native pot placed to receive it. When fresh from

Dense Forest and Sheer Hills

the tree, palm wine is, I am told—for I have never
had the courage to try it—a very refreshing beverage,
resembling in a way gingerbeer. If allowed to
stand and ferment it becomes sharp and sour, and
in that condition is intoxicating if taken in quantity.
It has been found by tests that the alcohol in palm
wine after fermentation is about equal to that in
beer, and it may be assumed, therefore, that the
intoxicating properties of the two are alike. Where
the palm tree does not exist an intoxicating drink
is made from maize, and further north, where maize
is not grown, from millet. It is a mistake to
suppose that intoxication was unknown among the
natives of West Africa until the merchant gave
them gin and rum, or that the work of the missionary has been baffled by the sale of these liquors.
My experience is, and I have seen the native far
inland and at places on the coast where contact
with the European is frequent, that there is very
little drunkenness among them, certainly nothing
to be compared with that to be met with in the
towns and villages of Christian England, and that
when intoxication occurs it is as often the result
of drinking palm wine as of gin or other imported
liquor.

I for one do not hold to the wild statements of

those who talk about the liquor traffic as if the sole object of the merchant was to intoxicate his customers, instead of giving them an alternative drink to their palm wine and the beverages made from maize and millet. There is not, I suppose, a people in the world without a manufactured stimulant of some kind, not necessarily for intoxicating purposes, although, as in the more civilised communities, it is at times so employed; and common sense tells one that, were the importation of liquor forbidden, the native would at once fall back upon his native beverages. By all means regulate if necessary the quality of the liquor imported, but why at the bidding of faddists prohibit or talk about prohibiting its importation altogether?

Our last halting-place before reaching Kumassi was Esumeja, a place which we were to hear more of later. It is a Bekwai village, and the chief of it, a fine, handsome youth, did all in his power to make us welcome, his demeanour being in marked contrast to the chiefs of the Adansi villages through which we had been travelling. He was very anxious to get to Kumassi before the Governor, as he had received the command of the King of Bekwai to be present with the other chiefs when

the Governor entered the town. So he asked permission to leave very early in the morning, and begged also that he might under the circumstances be excused from attendance when the Governor left, a duty which he said he would depute to his principal elder. He was off almost before dawn, as we knew from the awakening noise of horn-blowing and tom-tom beating.

CHAPTER III

WITH THE KINGS AT KUMASSI

SUNDAY, March 25th, was the day on which
we were to enter Kumassi with as much state
and ceremony as possible. How different was this
to the manner of our leaving it! The Acting
Resident met us at a village about two hours away
from Kumassi, and told us the programme for the
reception. We all smartened ourselves up at this
village, in order to make a good appearance when
entering the town, the Governor putting on
uniform, and the hammock-men clothes of blue
baft with drab facings, so that they should be
dressed alike and look smart. The pleasure shown
by the men with their new clothes was very amusing
to see, and they strutted about as if the whole place
belonged to them.

Nothing is to be seen of Kumassi until a bend
in the road brings you to the brow of a steep hill.
Here all the European officials met us and escorted
us into the town. A ricksha and a go-cart were

put at our disposal, and we changed from the hammocks into them. Down the hill the procession moved, and then after crossing a swamp by means of a causeway, and going up a shorter hill, the fort came into view.

Half-way up this shorter hill the procession halted, for here under a large shade tree were the Basel missionaries, headed by the Rev. F. and Mrs. Ramseyer, and all their school children. As the procession neared the spot the children commenced singing "God save the Queen," and it was pleasant to hear our beautiful National Anthem sung at a place where only a few years before human sacrifices and every horror of savagery had been enacted. The people gathered round as the children's voices invoked a blessing on our beloved Queen, but, alas! as we were soon to learn, they were not in unison with the sentiment, and many of those who were present had in their hearts a detestation of the white man and all his ways. Passing on again, the road took us under a triumphal arch, which, prettily decorated with palms, and having the one word "Welcome" on it, had been erected on the top of the hill. Then the fort came into full view, and a large and brilliant assembly of native kings, with their chiefs and

followers lining each side of the road leading up
to it.

It was a gorgeous pageant, this display of
potentates who had come into Kumassi from their
towns and villages to do honour to the Governor,
and through him to the Queen. What a farce it
all seems now to look back upon! For hatred and
rebellion were in their hearts, and this show of
loyalty was in most cases a mere pretence.

As we passed through the crowd each king rose
up from his native chair to salute the Governor.
Thousands of people were there, all looking with
seeming interest and pleasure at our arrival, and
the kings' umbrellas of state were made to proclaim
a welcome to us as we passed by, by being revolved
rapidly round and round, a native custom denoting
pleasure. Native drums were everywhere being
loudly beaten, and one of the kings—the King
of Mampon—had a drum and fife band, the
members of which were dressed in a pretence
of uniform. The fort was reached at length, and
here from the veranda we gazed upon a scene at
once animated and interesting, the surrounding
forest, with all its wealth of foliage, lending itself
as a fitting background to the primitive display.
Pretty did the scene then appear to us, but how

this selfsame forest was to pall upon us, and become to our minds the reverse of beautiful!

Without any delay the kings and chiefs formed into procession and, with their court officials and followers, walked past the fort to salute afresh the Governor, who stood upon the veranda bowing graciously to each as they defiled before him. The procession took more than an hour to pass by, and was indeed a gay and brilliant sight, an impressive display of barbaric grandeur. The kings, dressed in multi-coloured and gaudy robes of silk or velvet, and decked with solid gold ornaments of native workmanship in such profusion as to excite one's envy, were carried by in their palanquins. Each wore his crown of beaten gold and had his state umbrella held over him. On either side walked the court officials, carrying as their badges of office handsomely designed sticks or swords overlaid with gold, and around were pages in attendance, whose duty it was to wave enormous fans. Men followed behind bearing the kings' symbols of wealth and power in the shape of small boxes of native workmanship studded profusely with brass nails, or else big bunches of enormous keys. The boxes were supposed to be filled with gold dust and other valuables, but I imagine that they had nothing of the sort inside of them, for one fell into our hands later, and contained the most wonderful collection of rubbish I ever saw—old brass buttons, copper wire, a tag end of gold lace, and other trifles, and we searched in vain for anything of value. The glitter of the golden sticks of the linguists, for that is the title of the court officials carrying them, was quite dazzling.

The once-dreaded executioners were in the procession walking with sombre and staid demeanour, as if to emphasise the fact that their ancient glory had departed at the command of the Queen, before whose representative they were now defiling. The office of executioner is hereditary, so that in a great procession numbers of them would take part, some grey-headed and soon to enter the great unknown whither they had with such grim relish despatched hundreds or perhaps even thousands of victims, others lads and boys in their novitiate.

Then there were the court criers. Each of these important personages wore a cap made of the fur of the long-haired black monkey, which gave them a very fierce appearance quite befitting their position. On their bare breasts were handsome badges of fine-beaten gold hung round the neck with pure white cords.

It is not given to the native to do anything quietly, and the procession moved with as much noise as ceremony. One king—the King of Aguna —whom we were to be better acquainted with later on, coming near the veranda stepped out of his palanquin and executed a sort of *pas-de-seul*, which was indicative of his pleasure at meeting the Governor. So amid the continuous chattering of the assembled thousands, and the noise of beaten tom-toms and blowing horns, the procession moved along. The stationary guard of honour of Hausas, and four or five Maxim and other guns drawn up outside the fort, was a restful sight amid this moving mass, and enhanced the picturesqueness of the scene. How little did we then think that the aspect was so soon to change from gorgeous pageantry and outward peace to a turmoil of strife and jeopardy!

Later I heard from the King of Juabin, who throughout the rising stood by the Governor and remained loyal to the Queen, that just after he and his people had passed in procession before the Governor, a Kumassi chief named Kofi Kofia, who afterwards proved himself to be a ringleader of the rebels, came up to his palanquin and told him that if the Governor had not come to Kumassi to give them all a good message they intended to fight. This action on the part of Kofi Kofia was a gross breach of etiquette, for a king is too big a person to be approached except through one of his linguists, and considerable indignation was aroused by it. The King, not wishing to cause a commotion, contented himself with reporting the matter to the Acting Resident, who, however, very unfortunately treated it as of no consequence, with the result that the Governor only became aware of it days afterwards, when it was too late for the information to be of any service. The incident showed, I think, the state of feeling existing among the people, and proved that they were fully prepared, if the word were given, to break out into revolt.

The sun had set behind the forest trees before the Ashantis had all moved away, and left us liberty for much-needed rest. Our first night at Kumassi was by no means a pleasant one, for it was very hot, and all night through the sloths in the forest kept up their melancholy blood-curdling noise, challenging each other in the distance, and setting all sleep at defiance. These sloths were

With the Kings at Kumassi

always with us, and before long I found myself disliking them, more I was going to say, but certainly as much as I did the drumming which night after night went on in the rebel camps after they had been formed.

Fetishes play a very important part in the life of a native, and it was with a sinking heart that shortly after our arrival in Kumassi my servants told me that very bad fetishes had been passed on the road as we neared Kumassi, and that the sooner we left the place the better, for trouble was at hand. I dismissed the dismal thought, and made light of their statements, as everything was looking bright, and there was nothing to indicate that we were surrounded by malcontents, with hatred nursed and cherished for four years against the white man who had taken possession of their land, and had abolished all the savage customs which centuries had endeared to them, and age and use had consecrated. Slavery, human sacrifices, universal oppression, all had been swept away.

It may be interesting to say what form some of these bad fetishes seen on the road took. One was a fowl split open while still alive, and laid thus upon the fetish stone. This was seen at more than one fetish place as we passed. Another consisted

of strings of eggs fantastically twined about a fetish
house; and again there were knolls of earth pro-
truding into the road, and so formed as to represent
mounds over graves — a symbol that our party
would find burial in Ashanti, and that there would
be so many white men the less.

The Yam festival, as it is called, is perhaps the
greatest fetish function of the year. It is the time
when the firstfruits of the earth are presented to
the fetish priests, a ceremony corresponding in its
inception to our harvest festival. That it has no
further resemblance to it is clear from the following
account of a Yam festival held in Kumassi before
Ashanti came under the British flag, which is given
by the Rev. F. Ramseyer in his book, *Four Years
in Ashanti*.

"The preparation for the Yam festival now
began in earnest. All the public seats (dampans)
were whitened, the royal seats in the streets
entirely renewed. On the day of preparation for
the feast (December 14th) the King went through
the town to assure himself of the renewing of the
'dampans.' If the decorations had fallen, or the
roofs were leaking or patched, no notice was taken,
but the top must be well whitened. The procession
was more warlike than that of the preceding year.
Behind every chief the soldiers shouted a wild war

song, of which we often heard the words, 'if you
meet him, meet him to his destruction,' and they
beat time with their weapons held aloft. After the
King had greeted and honoured us with a bottle
of rum, he stepped across with some Mohammedans, who were awaiting him in the market-place
dressed in new bright attire. They held an ox,
the throat of which was now cut by the King.

"On the 16th the chiefs and warriors streamed
into the town more noisily than usual, and the
King's wives, decked with gold, their bodies be-
smeared with yellow-green powder, passed through
the streets without the men withdrawing. The
gigantic Prince of Mampon, sworn enemy of all
formality, shook hands with us heartily, while the
'brafo' and 'adumfo' (executioners) coloured red,
danced with long chains of jawbones round their
necks, which rattled like castinettes, drank something which looked like blood, and ate their feast
together out of a monstrous dish in the middle
of the reception-place. On the next day all laws
were abrogated, and everyone drinking freely was
permitted to do that which seemed good in his own
eyes. Even funerals were celebrated for those who
had suffered capital punishment.

"The great day was of course consecrated by a
festival offering, and any stray person at the palace
door might be suddenly attacked, slaughtered, and
divided between the 'brafos' and 'adumfos.' One
took a finger, another an arm or foot, and whoever

obtained the head danced in crazy ecstasy, painted its forehead red and white, kissed it on the mouth laughing or with mocking words of pity, and finally hung it round his neck or seized it with his teeth. Another took out the heart and roasted it, carried it in one hand and a loaf of maize bread in the other, and walked about as if he were eating his breakfast. The King, in common with his people, had disfigured his face with red stripes, and wore a black helmet, on which were engraved many golden crowns. The pomp and display on this occasion gave me a deeper impression of the riches of Ashantees than I had ever before received.

"In the evening they brought the skulls of their most important enemies from the mausoleum at Bantama, and placed them in the stillness of night in front of the fetish, solemnly enquiring after the state of their spirits. Amongst them was the skull of Sir Charles Macarthy, who was killed in the battle of Esamako in 1824, since kept in a brass basin covered with a white cloth. We did not see this, but we met some forty men, each bearing a skull in his hand, round the forehead of which a red rag was thrown, leaping, cursing, and jumping in the wildest confusion. The whole affair was the more distressing to us as it happened on a Sunday, and we thought of the change which might come over this land if Chistendom took the misery of such people more to heart.

"On the last day of the festival (December 22nd)

the King, before eating the new yams, washed himself in fetish water brought in bottles from distant springs sacred to the fetish. It was poured into basins wherein the chiefs performed frequent ablutions during the day, and they also sprinkled their chairs. On that occasion the King's wives were to be seen, so my wife went with our baby to one of the Dampans, when all crowded round us to look at the little one, calling her 'Amma Coomassie,' or 'the Saturday daughter of Coomassie," all girls being called after the day of the week on which they are born. ''Tis a miracle—they are children of the gods!' we heard them exclaiming, and often the enquiry, 'which is the wife?' was made, especially by the women, who could not take their eyes off little Rosa.

"The Queen mother was passing as we arrived with the glass and silver ornaments, followed by the eunuchs with the women. It appeared that the prohibition to look at them was again in force, for the men retired, and only a few Mohammedans were allowed to remain beside us. The ladies appeared in groups with a highly decorated leader at their head, which gave one the idea that the female part of the court was well organised. The favourites were dressed in silks, velvets, and gold ornaments, while others followed in more simple or even mean attire. Between the groups came eunuchs with little boys and girls who carried small boxes of playthings. The women had a long chewing-stick in their hands, so that they could rub their teeth when they pleased.

"The most richly ornamented was evidently the first wife, who in virtue of her dignity did not remove her stick from her mouth. Every age was represented, from young girls to grey-headed mothers, some of whom had been the wives of four or five kings. As we could scarcely distinguish the court ladies from the King's wives we cannot give their number, but it seemed as if those who went past with bowed heads were the real wives, and I counted from two hundred and fifty to two hundred and sixty of these, so that with invalids and others necessarily absent the total number cannot be less than three hundred ladies. That, however, is not known to any Ashantee. , These are kept in such good order by the eunuchs that I only saw one cast a stolen glance at our little Rosa, though doubtless they all wished to see the white baby. The King's eye beamed when he looked at her, as he turned to his people on both sides of his sedan, and pointed laughing to the babe on its mother's lap. This was a sign for hundreds of black heads to show us—shouting, laughing, and singing—their white teeth. His Majesty may well be proud, for none of his predecessors have ever been able to boast such white property, which will ever be spoken and sung of with great exultation throughout Ashantee, and evidently he thought much of the honour. His looking-glass which he always carried with him was on this occasion so large that two men could hardly stand upright under it. About seventy bearers of sheep followed, hundreds of which were slaughtered."

It did not take us long to visit the so-called places of interest in Kumassi. The King's palace practically existed no longer. The stone buildings of which it had been composed had been pulled down, and the stone—a very hard granite, which it is said had been brought all the way from the coast on the heads of slaves—used in the work of building the fort. Only a few mud huts remained, and these had been turned into a police station. There were still a few rude carvings to be seen on the walls, but the glory of the place had departed. The whole area and the buildings must have been very extensive once, but now the site is overgrown with long grass.

Then there was the fetish grove—the place into which the bodies of those slain for human sacrifices were thrown. It is on the left as Kumassi is entered from the south. Most of its trees were blown up with dynamite after the entry of the troops into Kumassi in 1896. The undergrowth of bush was then entirely cut away, and light was let into the whole of this once dark and gruesome place, where the ground had been strewn thick with human bones and skulls. These were all collected and buried, but even now when the rains are more than usually heavy, and the earth sinks, some of the latent horrors of the place appear in all their deformity.

Opposite to the fetish grove stands the fetish tree under which the executions took place. Most conveniently situated was this tree, for the fetish priests had not far to go to dispose of the bodies of their victims after the sacrifices had been made. The executioners must have had a busy time of it, because not only were victims required for every fetish custom and ceremony, but the punishment of death was inflicted for almost every penal offence. The victim always had the right of appealing to the King against his sentence ; but this had long been made a dead letter, because as soon as the sentence of execution had been proclaimed the victim was surrounded, and a sharp knife was run through one cheek, through the tongue, and so out of the other cheek, thus effectually preventing the person from uttering a single word. In fact, the poor wretch never escaped. At certain special festivals torture was resorted to before the victim was despatched, so as to afford amusement to the crowd assembled to see the execution.

I was much disappointed with the town of Kumassi, about which I had heard and read so much. The town as a town has ceased to exist. On the south-west there were, it is true, numerous huts, but these were inhabited by Fantis and other traders from the coast, who are swept into the one term "traders." Comparatively few huts inhabited by Kumassis remain, and these were all situated on the eastern side. To the north were the Basel Mission buildings, with their church and schoolhouse, and in the centre stand the fort and market-sheds, while on the ground between the fort and the Basel Mission Station were bungalows for the residence of Government officers, a hospital, prison, and house cantonments for the Hausas. The site of the town is a rib of hilly ground, the sides of which slope down to swamps which environ the town at all points. It was probably selected because of these swamps, which provide a sort of natural defence to the place. Beyond them are dense walls of forest and jungle, making one feel that the place is inclosed within prison walls. Right through the town and up to the suburb of Bantama, beyond the Basel Mission Station, runs a fine broad road forty

With the Kings at Kumassi

feet wide, and along the side of the eastern swamp is another good road, which passes across the marsh on a well-constructed causeway, and skirts a hill on which stands, or rather stood, for the rebels burnt it to the ground, the Wesleyan Mission House, and so leads northwards to Kintampo, the base depôt and station of the northern territories. There are many other roads from the town of less importance.

We visited the Basel Mission House, and found it most comfortable, and its garden lovely. Such roses and flowers I had not feasted my eyes upon since leaving England, and vegetables were as well grown, and in their usefulness as beautiful, as the flowers. There were Basel missionaries living here, and doing what they could to bring small Ashantis to see the errors of their forbears. Two of the missionaries were Mr. Ramseyer and his wife, whom I have already mentioned, and who, in 1871, were taken prisoners by the Ashantis and kept in captivity in Kumassi for four weary years before release came. It was most interesting to hear Mrs. Ramseyer recount some of her adventures during those four years. She told me that after the first few months they were fairly well treated by the King, and were released from the chains in which they had been kept since they were brought to Kumassi. The King was very delighted and proud when her little girl was born, saying that now Kumassi had something good in it. But their trials must have been very great, and it was strange that after the dearest wish of their hearts had been fulfilled — namely, to return to Kumassi under the British flag and work amongst the people—they should again have to face in that place anxiety and trouble, and again have to leave it with their lives trembling in the balance.

Bantama, a small village about fifteen minutes' walk from Kumassi, is a place of historic interest. It was here that the kings and royal personages were buried, and the village was on that account held sacred. The mausoleum has disappeared, having been destroyed upon the British occupation of Kumassi in 1896. Some of the village, too, had vanished in the general destruction, most of the natives having migrated into the bush villages around Ashanti, with those whose houses in Kumassi had been pulled down to provide a site for the fort, or to clear and ventilate the town. We saw a few Mohammedans and natives sitting about under the shade trees, and failed to find any indication that the place had once been the scene of many cruelties and tortures.

With the Kings at Kumassi

Mr. Ramseyer says in his book :—

"The most dreadful of the Ashantee festivals, Bantama or 'death wake,' now approached. The King went early in the morning of February 5th to Bantama, where the remains of his deceased predecessors were preserved in a long building approached by a gallery and partitioned into small cells, the entrances of which were hung with silken curtains. In these apartments reposed the skeletons of the kings fastened together with gold wire and placed in richly ornamented coffins, each being surrounded by what had given him most pleasure during his life. On this occasion every skeleton was placed on a chair in his cell to receive the royal visitor, who on entering offered it food, after which a band played the favourite melodies of the departed. The poor victim selected as a sacrifice, with a knife thrust through his cheeks, was then dragged forward and slain, the King washing the skeleton with his blood. Thus was each cell visited in turn, sacrifice after sacrifice being offered till evening closed ere the dreadful round was completed. We had heard the blowing of horns and beating of drums throughout the day, and were told that nearly thirty men had been slain. These, alas! were not all, for at six o'clock the King had returned, the horn and drums again sounded, betokening that more victims were yet to fall, and far into the night the melancholy sound

continued. Two blasts of the horn signified
'Death!' 'Death!' three beats of the drum,
'Cut it off!' and a single beat from another drum
announced 'The head has dropped.' Powerless
as we were, amid the fearful darkness around, to
hinder such atrocities, we could only sigh, and
pray that our captivity might bring about a better
state of things."

The fort in which we were to pass so many
weeks is a fine square building with rounded
bastions at the four corners. On each of these
bastions is a platform upon which can be placed
and worked a Maxim or other gun, and each gun
is protected by a roof raised on wooden supports ;
the space between the supports is filled in with
shutters which can be easily pulled up towards
the roof or, when there is rain, let down and
fastened. On the south side is the only entrance
to the fort, and here are heavy iron bullet-proof
gates which, when necessary, are kept closed by
the insertion of heavy beams resting in slots in
the wall on either side. On this side also are the
quarters allotted to the Résident, known as the
Residency. All along the front, almost up to
the bastions, runs a roofed veranda supported on
pillars planted outside the fort.

The quarters, which are very good and comfortable, consist of four rooms. Below, on the ground floor, are guard-rooms, one on either side of the entrance, and at the back of them two fair-sized rooms, one of which is used as the Treasury, and the other by the Resident as his dining-room. On the east and north sides, between the bastions, are brick-built covered sheds, each with store-rooms for warlike stores, and gun platforms. The walls of the fort are loopholed, and inside are platforms to make the loopholes available. All around the walls on the inside are convenient sheds, which, without interfering with the use of the loopholes, afford accommodation to as large a body of men as the safety of the fort against a savage foe demands; and in the centre of the inside square, formed by the four walls of the fort, is a large building divided into offices and store-rooms for provisions. In one corner is a well from which very good water is obtained. With plenty of food and ammunition, if the health of the occupants of the fort remained good, there would, I have been told, be no difficulty in holding it indefinitely against any number of natives. The ground is well cleared all around the fort, and while the garrison is on the alert it would be impossible for an enemy to cross the open in sufficient numbers to prove dangerous.

CHAPTER IV

A MOMENTOUS PALAVER

THE durbar, or palaver as it is called in West Africa, at which the Governor was to meet the assembled kings and chiefs, had been arranged for the 29th March. Everything was to be carried out with all possible ceremony on the open parade ground in front of the fort. A canopy had been erected, under which the Governor and his principal officials were to sit, the kings sitting on their tribal stools in a semicircle facing the canopy, with their respective chiefs and court officials ranged behind them. Long before the hour fixed for the palaver the kings were to be seen coming to the parade ground, some on foot, others borne in their palanquins. All were attired in costly robes of silk, and wore the golden ornaments denoting their high rank and position. Native Government officers had been told off to show them to their places, care having been taken to allot positions to them in accordance with their precedence. A guard of

A Momentous Palaver

honour marched out of the fort and took up a
prominent place behind the chairs which had been
placed for the Governor and his officers, and close
to the flagstaff from which was waving the Union
Jack.

Punctually at the hour fixed the Governor,
dressed in the uniform of his rank, and wearing
the collar and order of St. Michael and St. George,
left the fort, accompanied by all the European
officers, those who held military rank being dressed
in uniform. The guard presented arms, and the
kings and chiefs stood up as the Governor and his
suite walked to their places. I was allowed to be
present, and had a seat allotted to me in the background, and the Basel missionaries had been invited to attend. To do honour to the occasion
I had donned my smartest gown. It may seem
out of place to chronicle our dress, but I do so
in order to contradict the false statements that
have appeared to the effect that the palaver was
conducted without ceremony, and that the Governor
wore an old shooting coat! The person from whom
that story emanated can have but a small acquaintance with truth, or must possess a highly imagina-
tive brain. I had previously seen one or two
palavers of perhaps less importance, all conducted

A Momentous Palaver

with the ceremonial which native custom demands, but I have never seen one more impressive or more ceremonious than that at which I was then permitted to be present.

The Governor, having taken his seat, addressed the assembly, the interpreter standing at his right hand, and translating each sentence as it was spoken into native language. It cannot be an easy matter to address an assembly of natives, because the English must be of the very simplest, so that the interpreter may himself grasp the meaning of it, and thus be able to repeat each sentence with full force in the native tongue and idiom. All the kings and chiefs listened with grave attention. In all the vast crowd not a sound was heard. The salient points of the address appeared to be these—that the Ashanti kings must recognise the Queen of England as the paramount power in their land, and that in connection with the maintenance of peace, order, and the development of the country for the people's good, it was expected that they would hereafter make an annual payment towards the expenses of the Government.

Referring to the first point, the Governor said he understood that while many hoped for the return of Prempeh, others desired to see his old rival, Atcheriboanda, who for some years had been living under surveillance at Accra, brought back to the country and installed as King Paramount; that neither of these two events must be looked for, and that the powers and privileges attaching to the paramount power would be wielded by the Queen's representative on the Gold Coast, and in his behalf by the Resident at Kumassi. In connection with the second point, the Governor, after referring to the treaty signed at Fomena in 1874, in which the Ashantis had agreed to pay 50,000 ounces of gold as an indemnity, but had failed to do so, and to the expenses incurred in connection with the expedition of 1896, reminded the kings that they had hitherto not been made to carry out their treaty obligation, or to make good the expenses of the 1896 expedition, because the Queen was desirous that the people of Ashanti should become accustomed to a settled form of Government; that even now there was to be no arbitrary demand for an immediate payment, but that each tribe must contribute an annual sum in the way of interest, in accordance with its means, as laid down by Ashanti custom in times past.

This speech, which was in all respects careful and temperate, has been made the subject of

A Momentous Palaver

misrepresentation in the Press. It has been said that the Governor demanded the delivery of the golden stool, and insolently claimed to be regarded as the king paramount of Ashanti. This is again absolutely untrue. I have mentioned what was said with regard to the exercise of the powers of the paramount authority; and with regard to the golden stool, the Governor said that the Queen, being now the paramount power, should have the stool belonging to that power as the symbol of her supremacy. He added that the kings were sitting upon their tribal stools, and that he hoped they would evince their loyalty by producing the golden stool and handing it over, not, of course, for him to sit upon, as was recorded by this calumnious correspondent, but to show their recognition of the Queen's position.

As soon as the Governor had finished his address, the usual native custom of hand-shaking commenced. The kings, with their chiefs and suite, filed past and shook hands with the Governor. In this procession were the King of Mampon, by native custom the senior king of the Ashanti Confederation, the Kings of Bekwai, Kokofu, Juabin, Adansi, Aguna, Nkwanta, Kumawu, Bompata, and several others, as well as the Queen of Ejisu, who later became notorious on account of the leading part which she and her tribe took in the rising against British rule. The only absentees were the King of Nkoranza, a tribe far away to the north of Ashanti, and the Queen of Ofinsu, who it was stated was too old to travel.

There were also the principal chiefs of the all-powerful Kumassi tribe, whose king at this time was with others in exile at Sierra Leone. Headed by the three members of the Native Committee—a triumvirate formed in 1896 upon the deportation of Prempeh and the occupation of Ashanti, for the purpose of acting as a board of advisers upon native questions, and of discharging such duties as the Resident might relegate to them—they too made their way past the Governor's chair. None betrayed a sign of disaffection, and the Queen of Ejisu, when her turn came, stopped before the Governor, and, stretching out her hand, examined the order and decoration which he was wearing, requesting the interpreter to say that they looked very nice, and that she admired his uniform. Then turning round, she insisted on coming up to my chair and shaking me by the hand, with the result that my new pair of gloves was soiled and spoilt.

A Momentous Palaver

To each king as he shook hands the Governor spoke a few words, and with the conclusion of this ceremony the palaver came to an end. The Governor and his officials rose from their seats, the guard presented arms, and the kings and chiefs retired without having given any indication that there were clouds on the horizon.

CHAPTER V

RIVALS FOR A TRIBAL STOOL

IN West Africa there are nearly always one or more petty tribal disputes on hand, which not unfrequently are a source of anxiety to the Government, and require very delicate handling. A dispute of this sort had arisen in Ashanti, and was one of the matters which the Governor hoped to settle during his stay. As I happened to be a spectator of the negotiations, and of the placing of the selected king on the tribal stool, which was a most interesting ceremony, I will record what I saw. The Ashantis include many tribes, each having its king, the King of the Kumassi tribe being by native custom the King Paramount, and by virtue of that position entitled to sit upon the golden stool.

It was the Nsuta tribe in which the dispute arose. The matter had been referred by the disputants to the Acting Resident for arbitration, but he had

KING OF MAMPON, WIVES, AND ATTENDANTS

Face page 84

Rivals for a Tribal Stool

failed to bring about an understanding, and had under the circumstances reported the matter to headquarters. The case had reached a somewhat acute stage when we arrived at Kumassi. Both claimants with their respective followers were in the town, and the settlement of the matter was urgent, for ill feeling had arisen, and the work of keeping the peace between them was daily becoming more difficult. I recollect seeing the two parties on the day of the durbar. They both sat together on that occasion as belonging to the same tribe, and I was struck with the different appearance which each side presented. One of the claimaints, named Kwabina Ntem, was a fine, intelligent-looking man; he was very handsomely dressed, being clothed in expensive satin and silk cloths, and having massive gold rings on his fingers and toes and a gold chain round his neck. The chiefs supporting him were also well and handsomely dressed, their followers being supplied with expensive and showy regalia, and the whole party was conspicuous by its display, and by the courtly deference shown to Kwabina Ntem. The rival party, on the other hand, headed by Kwasi Berekum, seemed desirous of accentuating its indifference to outward show, and to wish to suggest that their claims to recognition rested less on this than on intrinsic merit.

The day following the durbar was fixed for the first hearing of the case. Both parties arrived before the appointed hour, and took up their allotted places in the courtyard of the fort. There were present also the three members of the Native Committee. These three assessors require a passing word, for two, at least, were disloyal, and took leading parts in the rising against British rule.

Opoku Mensa, the senior member, was a tall, fine-looking man, his face full of intelligence, though constantly relapsing into the usual Ashanti indifference, or apparent lack of knowledge of the subject in hand. Nantchwi, the second member, had all the appearance of an Israelite, with heavy features, and a thick beard covering his cheeks and chin; he sat next to Opoku Mensa. The third member was Efilfa, a man with a crafty, forbidding face, an Ashanti of the Ashantis, for he was one of the chiefs of the Kumassi tribe, and a man whom to see was to distrust. How he ever came to be selected for a position which demanded loyalty and straightforward action struck me as curious. However, there he was, and it did not appear to me likely that he would facilitate the settlement of the dispute.

The hearing of the case might, I knew, occupy two or three days, because the natives invariably think it necessary to talk about all sorts of irrelevant matter, and this was a question in which irrelevancy was very sure to be rampant. My husband told me that, apart from the usual discursiveness, both parties through their respective chiefs (for it is not etiquette for the men to speak themselves) stated their cases with commendable fairness.

Both the claimants were of royal descent, and based their claims on right of birth. It was, however, very apparent that Kwasi Berekum was somewhat deficient in intellect, and it was on that account not unlikely that his selection for the tribal stool had caused umbrage to the chiefs who had decided against him, and who, objecting to the rulership being in the hands of such a man, had set up a rival in Kwabina Ntem. It was found that Kwabina Ntem's claim by right of birth was not so good as Kwasi Berekum's, but it was clear that he had the stronger party and the most influential chiefs on his side, with one exception. It was just possible, under the circumstances, that if another

Rivals for a Tribal Stool

scion of the royal house could be found, a man of intelligence and presence, both claimants might be induced to resign in his favour. This was the situation as it appeared after the first day's hearing ; Kwasi Berekum's party upon being approached in the matter, expressed themselves as quite willing to select another candidate, and Kwasi Berekum himself offered no objection to retirement, if thereby the unity of the tribe could be secured. Yow Mafo was suggested as a suitable candidate. Kwabina Ntem's party was next sounded. Yow Mafo was, they said, unobjectionable, but they preferred Kwabina Ntem. There seemed to be some chance of securing the adoption of Yow Mafo, and another formal meeting was held. All the chiefs attended as before, with the exception of Efilfa, the third member of the Kumassi Native Committee, who excused himself on the ground of ill-health, but who was, it was subsequently discovered, actively engaged in organising the forces of rebellion.

My husband announced at this meeting that, having given the whole matter very careful consideration, it appeared to him best, in order to secure a general agreement, that the claims of Kwasi Berekum and Kwabina Ntem to the stool should be set aside in favour of a third party, who

Rivals for a Tribal Stool

would command the confidence of the whole tribe. Yow Mafo was then suggested as a suitable man to elect. Asked if they would agree to his election, Kwasi Berekum's party replied in the affirmative, while Kwabina Ntem's party asked for time to consider the proposal, the members of the Kumassi Native Committee expressing their opinion in favour of the arrangement. The meeting was adjourned until the afternoon, when Kwabina Ntem's party promised to be ready with their answer. Everything appeared to be going well, and making for the desired settlement; but, alas! Kwabina Ntem announced as the result of the deliberation that he was not prepared to relinquish his claims.

My husband, it appears, was not unprepared for this contingency. I remember his telling me how the matter stood, and that, if Kwabina Ntem maintained his position, he had another proposal to make. It was this : that Yow Mafo should be elected King, and that Kwabina Ntem should stand "next to the stool," as, in accordance with native custom, the position is called, and be elected King upon the death of Yow Mafo. Accordingly, when Kwabina's party proved recalcitrant, this further suggestion was put forward. Again time was asked

Rivals for a Tribal Stool

for consideration. In the meantime, Opoku Mensa had suggested that the influence of the King of Mampon, the senior of the kings of the tribes forming the Ashanti Confederation, should be brought to bear upon Kwabina Ntem, so as to secure his assent to the proposal, which, short of placing him on the stool, was one obviously in his favour.

So matters stood when the first signs of a rising of the Ashantis against British rule began to be apparent. The King of Mampon held many meetings with Kwabina Ntem and his party, but finally reported failure, and stated at the same time that if a general rising took place, he doubted if the Nsutas supporting Kwabina Ntem would stand by the Government. I must not forget to mention that, as soon as it became clear that the negotiations as to the disputed succession were likely to be protracted, my husband insisted upon the surrender of the tribal stools, and, wrapped up in fine native cloths, they were brought into the fort. In the end the question was settled by Kwabina Ntem and his party going over to the rebels, while Yow Mafo and his party remained with us. I saw Yow Mafo many times after this. He was a fine young fellow and had an intelligent look; but although he fought bravely for the Government on more

than one occasion, I somehow never quite took
to him.

Kwabina Ntem's departure was the signal for an
outburst from the loyal King of Aguna. It appears
that all the handsome gold ornaments worn by
Kwabina Ntem in order to make a favourable impression at the meeting, had been borrowed by him
for the purpose from the King of Aguna, and that
when he left Kumassi suddenly he neglected to
return them. Many a time did the King of Aguna
talk to me of his lost ornaments, and rail against
Kwabina Ntem, not for his disloyalty to the
Government, but for his dishonesty.

Later, during the siege of Kumassi, the loyal
kings pressed for the recognition of Yow Mafo as
King of the Nsuta tribe, and for his instalment on
the stool. This request was granted, and a great
and impressive ceremony took place in the courtyard of the fort. When the loyal kings and such
of their people as were with them had seated themselves in royal robes on their tribal stools, Yow
Mafo, led by his supporting chiefs, was presented
to each in turn as the person whom the Government approved for election. This being done, the
stool of Nsuta and all the subsidiary stools of the
tribe were arranged for the ceremony of blessing

them. The spirits of departed Nsuta kings were called and begged to witness the selection of Yow Mafo as a worthy successor. It was prayed that all the virtues of the departed kings might descend upon him, and that it might be given to him to rule over the tribe with discretion, not abating any of its past glories. but adding to them if opportunity to do so were afforded. Each stool was then sprinkled by Yow Mafo with a libation of rum, and before each he vowed to be faithful to the tribe, and faithful to the British Government that had placed them in his hands. Finally he was led up to the principal stool by the King of Mampon, and placed upon it. He was evidently very pleased at his new position. Then getting up he made obeisance in turn to his brother kings present, namely the Kings of Mampon, Juabin, Nkwanta, and Aguna, to each of whom he vowed friendship and the alliance of the Nsuta tribe. While engaged in this act, his skin was smeared with a white adhesive powder, which, so far as I could judge, appeared to be a ceremony equivalent to that of anointing a king with oil. The function was now over, and it only remained for the new King to be presented to the Governor, who, seated for the purpose, had him brought up by the King of Mampon with all his

attendant chiefs and people, and after the presentation gave him some advice and counsel. After
this day, Yow Mafo was at least two inches taller,
and I never saw him without the smile of pleasure
which gladdened his face when he was formally
placed on the stool.

Twice, before we had to march out of Kumassi,
did he have to visit the tribal stools, which, for
safety, were kept in my husband's office, and make
vows over them, the occasions being the anni-
versaries of the deaths of former occupants. The
vows were of some length, and differed in the case
of each stool. Poor Yow Mafo stumbled over
them once or twice, although he had evidently
done his best to commit them to memory; but he
had a court official to prompt him when he failed,
and so he soon picked himself up again and went
on. The morning we left the fort he was very
anxious about the safety of the stools : he wanted
to take them with him, being fearful that if the fort
should fall into the hands of the rebels the stools
would pass over to Kwabina Ntem. My husband,
although very busy, listened to his plaint, and
having ascertained that he had not enough of his
own followers to carry all the stools, pointed out
the danger of taking them through the rebel lines,

suggesting that only the chief tribal stool should be taken. This satisfied Yow Mafo, and for the last time my husband, accompanied by Yow Mafo, re-entered the fort. The stool was taken out, and eventually reached the coast; but, alas! not with Yow Mafo. Poor Yow Mafo! he was never destined to rule over his tribe, and his vows and protestations uttered during the ceremony of enstoolment proved futile; for, worn out by the hardships and privations endured during the siege and the march from Kumassi, he died before he reached the coast, and was buried in a strange land, away from his people and far from his home. It was a sad ending to a promising career, and my husband much regretted the loss of so loyal a supporter of the Government as Yow Mafo promised to become.

CHAPTER VI

THE STORM GATHERS AND BREAKS

THE Governor had received information from a reliable source that the villages in the Atchima country, which are situated about two days' march from Kumassi, were more than well stocked with arms, gunpowder, and lead, and he had decided to ascertain if possible to what extent these warlike stores had been accumulated, as he regarded their storage in any quantity as a menace to the position of the Resident.

It was decided, after consultation with the Acting Resident, to despatch a small force of Hausas under two European officers, who should march through the villages and note the disposition of the people and the amount of stores which had been collected. This force, under the command of Captains Armitage and Leggett, marched away early on the morning of Saturday the 31st March, and made for Bali. It was in the neighbourhood of this Kumassi bush village—for Atchima is

The Storm Gathers and Breaks

inhabited by the Kumassi tribe—that the golden
stool was supposed to be kept. Bali was duly
reached, but the Hausas had not been there many
hours when the Kumassis, who had cleared out on
their arrival, returned fully armed and attacked
them. The attack was as unexpected as it was
severe, and the European officers had the greatest
difficulty in extricating the force, and bringing it
back to Kumassi. The Kumassis were evidently
out in large numbers, and at every available point
along the road delivered an attack. On Sunday
the Governor had heard that the Kumassis were
revolting and arming themselves, and endeavoured
to send a warning message, but the message failed
to reach the force, which on Wednesday returned
with a loss of two killed, one missing, and eighteen
wounded. This was the first time since 1873 that
the Ashantis had attacked a British force, and it
must be regarded as the commencement of the
rising.

We learnt afterwards that the Kumassi chiefs
had refused to attend a meeting called by the
Ashanti kings for the purpose of discussing what
had been said at the durbar, saying that the young
men of the tribe, disgusted at the country having
been given up in 1896 without resistance, and

The Storm Gathers and Breaks

anxious to shake off the British yoke, under which they were unable to employ slaves or to carry on their old fetish sacrifices, had determined to fight, whether they were supported by the other tribes or not. It was decided to attack the Governor's party on its way back to the coast, and, if possible, to take the Governor alive and keep him as a hostage for the return of Prempeh. It was argued that all the British troops were fighting in South Africa, and that there were none available to come to the Gold Coast to help the Governor, so that now was the time to strike for independence, and that success was certain. The despatch of the expedition into the Atchima country changed their plans. A determination was hurriedly made to attack the force on its way to Bali, for it was considered certain that if the force could be overwhelmed, Kumassi with the Governor and those remaining with him would easily fall into their hands before reinforcements from the coast could arrive.

The pent-up storm had burst. As a rule coming events cast their shadows before them, but no such signs had been discerned by the authorities in Ashanti, and the Governor was suddenly confronted with a rising the extent of which he had yet to discover. It might be that the rising would be confined, as at first appeared to be the case, to the Kumassi tribe; or, on the other hand, most or all of the Ashanti tribes might place themselves in revolt. It was a difficult situation to deal with, and one that must have taxed to the utmost the brains and stout hearts of those who had to unravel it. We were one hundred and fifty miles away from help, in a climate notoriously unhealthy, especially in the rainy season now close at hand, and amid a people warlike, uncivilised, and barbarous. My heart failed me. I dared not think of what might happen. The Governor lost no time in grappling with the serious difficulties with which he was confronted. The telegraph wires were set in motion, and all available troops were ordered up from the coast and from the northern territories, where the bulk of the Hausa force had for some time been employed. Then the extent of the rising and causes of disaffection had to be ascertained. For this latter purpose the kings and chiefs who had attended the durbar were summoned. All attended with the exception of the Kings of Adansi and Bekwai and the Queen of Ejisu, who had obtained permission to leave for their respective countries after the conclusion of

The Storm Gathers and Breaks

the durbar. It was found that the rising was not altogether confined to the Kumassis, as they had already been joined by the Ejisus and Ofinsus. The kings present protested their loyalty to the Queen, and maintained that their tribes would not join in the revolt. Thus matters looked a little brighter than had appeared at the outset, and the Governor hoped that by employing the loyal kings to negotiate with the malcontents it might be possible to persuade them to abandon their hostile attitude, especially when they found that several powerful tribes had no intention of joining them, and that the revolt would not be universal.

The Acting Resident from the first made light of the revolt, assuring the Governor that there was nothing to be alarmed about. The Ashantis, he said, were strange people, and often showed their teeth in various ways, and he was certain that things would quiet down as they had done before. This was by no means the view taken by the Governor, who, I remember, was much annoyed to hear about this time that there had been an apprehended rising five months back, in November, of which he had never been advised. I learnt later, from a conversation with the Basel missionaries, that at that time things had looked so

The Storm Gathers and Breaks

bad they had been warned to be ready to move into the fort upon the receipt of a summons to do so from the Residency. Yet when matters quieted down no report was made, and the Governor was allowed to go to Kumassi without a suspicion that there was or had been anything wrong.

On Sunday, April the 1st, Kumassi showed a very deserted appearance. Chiefs Nantchwi and Efilfa, members of the Native Committee, had left to join the rebel forces now forming a camp across the swamp to the eastward of the town, and only the loyal kings and their followers, as well as certain of the chiefs of Kumassi who had dissented from the decision to revolt, remained. Chief Obuabasa, or Opoku Mensa, as he was more generally called, the senior member of the Native Committee, had, as transpired afterwards, warned the Acting Resident that his colleagues meditated flight, but his warning was disregarded and not reported, and the opportunity of arresting these influential persons before they could give trouble to the Government was lost.

During the afternoon, looking out along the road leading to Bantama, I saw a crowd of people coming along with loads on their heads. As they came nearer it was seen that the Basel missionaries,

The Storm Gathers and Breaks

alarmed at the situation, had packed up all their worldly goods, and with their people were hastening to the fort for protection. They were, however, induced to return, and a guard of Hausas was stationed in close proximity to the mission premises in order to give them 'confidence.

Every day the loyal kings of Mampon, Juabin, Aguna, and Kumawu' met the Ashanti chiefs for the purpose of inducing them to desist from revolt, and to lay their grievances before the Governor in palaver. It was a period of great anxiety to us all. Sometimes the meetings were very stormy, as when the Queen of Ejisu charged the King of Mampon with double-dealing. Poor King of Mampon! He was evidently not a man of strong character, and must have had a very difficult task in following the Governor's advice, and remaining loyal to the Queen. At last the negotiations came to an abrupt end. The malcontents sent in a list of insolent demands, which if accepted would, they said, lead them to lay down their arms, and put an end to hostilities. The terms stated were not such as could be accepted, and the loyal kings were told that the negotiations must be broken off. It was now to be war with all its horrors, and we knew what that meant to us who, weak in numbers, were in the midst of an implacable and savage foe. But the British flag had to be guarded, and no one flinched from the task.

During the negotiations stock had been taken of the provisions and warlike stores in the fort, and additional stores had been telegraphed for. The telegraph wires had been cut, but as yet the road to Prahsu had not been closed, and messengers were able to get through. Indeed, so leisurely were the rebels in their movements that they did not oppose representatives of the Ashanti Goldfields Corporation coming to Kumassi to interview the Governor upon mining matters, nor did they molest them when they left on Wednesday, the 18th April. With them left the Acting Resident, who still maintained that all would settle down peaceably, and had received permission to quit his post and proceed to England on leave.

The first detachment of Hausa troops from Accra was expected to arrive on the 18th April. They were impatiently looked for, and to our great delight arrived at four o'clock, when they received a warm welcome. They had not encountered any opposition on the road, and we thought that perhaps after all the malcontents would not try conclusions with us, but we were soon undeceived. The attendance of the people at the market with foodstuffs began to fall off, and soon ceased altogether, and it was found that messengers sent down the road with letters or telegrams could not get through, but had to return. The road was being closed, and the isolation and siege of Kumassi were imminent.

It was at this time that the discovery was made that the young King of Kokofu, who had expressed his loyalty to the Queen and had remained in Kumassi, had been in communication with the malcontents. They had promised that if he and his tribe would join them, they would place him upon the golden stool as King Paramount of Ashanti until such time as the exiled Prempeh should come to his own again. The King was, through intermarriage, of royal Kumassi lineage, as well as a scion of the royal line of Kokofu, and so was, in accordance with native custom, eligible for the stool. He was a proud, arrogant lad, whose conduct had alienated the love and respect which the chiefs of his tribe would otherwise have shown to him, and it was through one of them that his double-dealing came to light. He and his people were living in that part of Kumassi which abuts on the Cape Coast road, and is known locally as

The Storm Gathers and Breaks

Asafu. Here a picket had been placed to watch the approach to the town. It was posted close to the royal hut, and orders were given that the King's movements were to be carefully watched and reported.

A few days later it appeared evident-that the King contemplated flight. The Governor on learning this at once had the guard increased and arrangements made for his arrest. It was the work of a few minutes, and before anyone knew definitely what had happened the King had been carried up in a hammock and lodged in the fort. There he remained until necessity drove us to force our way to the coast, when he accompanied the column, and was deported to Sierra Leone.

In order to keep open the road which is known as the Cape Coast Road, the Governor had sent messages to the King of Bekwai claiming his assistance, and requesting him to co-operate by sending his fighting men to join the troops and loyal kings at Kumassi. He sent two of his linguists with a small bodyguard of thirty armed men, with the reply that his loyalty could be reckoned upon, but that he feared that if he sent his fighting men out of Bekwai his neighbours and hereditary enemies, the Adansis, would at once

overrun the country and devastate his villages. This was the first definite intimation of the disloyalty of the Adansis. It was not, however, unexpected by the Governor. Recognising at once that it would be best, having regard to the necessity for safeguarding the mines and property of the Ashanti Goldfields Corporation at Obuassi, that the Bekwais should remain in their country and hold the Adansis in check until reinforcements could arrive from the coast, the Governor sent back word that he approved the King's action under the circumstances.

With the detachment which had arrived at Kumassi on the 18th April came Captain Middlemist, the Deputy Inspector-General of Gold Coast Constabulary, who was at once placed in military command, and, a sufficient force being now available, it was considered desirable to harass the rebels and make them feel that they had to reckon with an active foe. Expeditions were sent out for the purpose of dispersing the rebels, destroying their villages and camps, and generally keeping them on the move until the force at command had been rendered sufficiently strong by reinforcements to admit of their being decisively engaged. Two of these expeditions were successful,

The Storm Gathers and Breaks

but the third detachment nearly met with a serious disaster. The guide took the column in a wrong direction, and landed it in the very centre of the rebels. A sharp fight ensued, during which one native officer and three men were killed, while no less than fifty-three were wounded. This engagement made it quite clear that the Kumassis and their allies were fully armed, and had plentiful supplies of ammunition. The officers who were with the force told me afterwards that the fusillade was incessant, and that but for the fact that the rebels took no aim and fired high there would have been few of them able to return and tell the tale. We learnt later that most of the ammunition in the hands of the rebels had been collected with the object of opposing the expedition to Kumassi in 1896, but that as it was decided to offer no resistance it had not then been used. Much had, it seems, been collected about two years after the deportation of Prempeh, when the malcontent Ashantis took an oath that they would fight at the first available opportunity.

I have been told that it is one of the superstitions of the country that if a big man, such as a king or chief, is taken prisoner without blood being shed, the fighting men of the tribe are disgraced and put

The Storm Gathers and Breaks

under a ban until they can right themselves in the eyes of their people. No blood had been shed at the taking of Prempeh, which the Ashantis regarded as having been done unfairly, that is, not in fair fight, and it has been stated that soon after his deportation a fetish oath was taken by the Kumassis to be avenged upon the white man for thus taking their king without firing a shot.

CHAPTER VII

HEMMED IN BY SAVAGE HORDES

WEDNESDAY, April 25th, was the day on which the rebels became actively hostile in and around Kumassi.

On the evening of the 24th April we went for a short walk. Everywhere there was depression and dreariness. The few Kumassis still in the town, who had not then decided what they would do, looked sullen and stubborn, and I was right glad when the walk was over and we were in the fort again. Sitting on the veranda, I remember remarking to my husband that the stillness and depression over everything seemed like a calm before a storm. We little thought then what the next day would bring forth, and how changed would be the scene upon which we were then looking.

On the morning of the 25th things seemed as usual, but about 9 a.m. the first note of warning was sounded by a letter from the Basel Mission

Hemmed in by Savage Hordes

signed by Mr. Ramseyer, saying that the Ashantis had closed in nearer to his house during the night, and he feared that they meditated an attack. This letter was followed immediately by another, saying that his water carriers had as usual gone for water, and that they had been captured by the rebels and one or two of them murdered. Captain Middlemist, finding that the foe were threatening Bantama, sent word to the Basel missionaries to quit their premises and come to the fort. At first they were placed in the officers' quarters near the cantonments, but later in the day, when these were seriously threatened, they were withdrawn to the fort, where they remained until our departure from Kumassi on the 23rd of June.

It soon became apparent that the rebels intended to be aggressive. A Maxim gun was run out of the fort, and posted so as to command the road leading to the fort from Bantama, and later a 7-pounder gun was sent for, but these failed to check the advance of the Ashantis, and had ultimately to be withdrawn.

By midday Bantama was occupied by the Ashantis, who gradually forced back all the outposts, and were thus able to take possession of the whole of Kumassi with the exception of the fort, and the ground immediately around it within range of the guns. It was a terrible day; the firing was incessant. Our troops were steady and well in hand, but overwhelmed by the immense numbers against them. While the fight proceeded the scene around the fort was one that it is almost impossible to describe. The loyal inhabitants of Kumassi at the first alarm had vacated their huts and houses, and poured in crowds to the fort seeking protection under its walls. The wives and children of the Hausa soldiers came from the cantonments; the Fantis and others from their part of the town, and the Mohammedans from their settlement on the outskirts of Kumassi, added themselves to the general panic. All brought with them their portable worldly possessions. Within half an hour of the alarm caused by the firing there was on all sides of the fort a seething mass of humanity.

All knew that they would be made short work of were they to fall into the hands of the rebels —the loyal because they were loyal; the Mohammedan because he was a stranger in the land, trading, making money, and generally ignoring the native rights and customs of the people among whom he found himself; the Fantis and others from the coast because they were interlopers doing business under the protection of the British Government. Altogether there were upwards of three thousand men, women, and children gathered together, most of them thoroughly panic-stricken, while others seemingly callous, or looking at events from the lighter and brighter side, were endeavouring to make the best of the situation. It was a pitiful sight, but nevertheless I found an interest amid all the turmoil and excitement in watching the assembly growing bigger and bigger, and gradually compressing. Those first on the scene located themselves close under the wall, and this proved later a very great advantage, for its shelter afforded some protection from the weather.

Throughout the morning the fort gates had been left open, a small guard only being kept in front of them to prevent the ingress of refugees. But as the day wore on it became evident that it would not be possible with our comparatively small force to beat back the swarms of Ashantis attacking us, and that in order to afford protection to the refugees there must be concentration on the fort. The gradual retirement of the Hausas caused further panic among the refugees, and it was seen that they meditated rushing the gates, so as to get inside the fort. Gradually the gate guard was removed one by one, and then came the work of suddenly shutting the gates and barricading them. The first movement to close them was the signal for a rush by the refugees.

Never shall I forget the sight. My heart stood still, for I knew that were this panic-stricken crowd to get in, the fort would fall an easy prey to the rebels, and we should be lost. It was an anxious moment. Could the guard close the gates in face of that rushing multitude? A moment later and the suspense was over. The gates had been closed after a desperate struggle, and the refugees fell back. This I soon realised, because, seeing that admittance by the gates was hopeless, the refugees began to climb up the posts of the veranda, determined to gain their end by passing through our quarters. Sentries had then to be stationed on the veranda to make them go down again quicker than they came up. I felt very much for these poor people, but, besides the fact that the fort would not have accommodated a third of them, the whole space was wanted for the troops and for defensive purposes.

By five o'clock the troops had been withdrawn from outlying points, and now formed a cordon

Hemmed in by Savage Hordes

round the refugees, ready with the assistance of the fort guns to repel attack. Hitherto the rebels had refrained from coming out into the open, but emboldened by their success they abandoned caution, and advancing, challenged us on all sides. However, they were at once to find that the game was not a paying one, for the machine guns were brought to bear upon them with effect, making known to them that they were not quite as smooth and placid as they looked shining in the bastions of the fort.

As night and the darkness came on firing ceased, and the rebels withdrew. The poor tired officers and men must have been thankful, for it had been a hard day and a dispiriting one for all of us. The rebels, not content with the day's work, began to set fire to the huts in the Hausa cantonments and other parts of the town. It was an awful scene. Tongues of fire were leaping up to the skies on all sides and lighting up the horrors of the scene around, adding emphasis to the stern and terrible reality of all we had gone through.

Can anyone imagine what that night meant to us—the agony of mind, and the effort to work out the problem of how we were to meet the many and great difficulties which now stared us in the face?

Hemmed in by Savage Hordes

The noise made by the refugees passes all conception; the incessant chatter, chatter of this multitude cannot be imagined, and certainly cannot be described. Children yelling and squealing played their little part in the general tumult; but throughout our Hausa troops maintained their posts around the fort, and all, both inside and out, were on the alert to do their duty. It seemed to me that the night would never pass, and the daylight, when it came, was greeted with joy, as all hoped that in occupation some relief might be found from the terrible oppression of that incessant noise.

Thursday, the 26th, dawned, and we wondered what our fate would be that day. Everyone was early on the move, for an attack was expected at daybreak. As it turned out the rebels left us alone, but we could see them running hither and thither in the cantonments and across the roads, very busy and active, and we wondered what they were doing.

Later in the day a strong escort of Hausas was sent to the hospital to recover if possible the drugs and medical stores which, through lack of carriers to do the work of removal, had been abandoned when the sick were brought into the fort. The

A STREET IN KUMASSI

Face page 120

rebels must have regarded the hospital with a fetish reverence, for they had only taken away the doors and a few boards, leaving the drugs and stores untouched. Great was our joy on recovering all these precious things, for although we had a reserve supply in the fort, we could not tell how long they would have to last us, and all stores were now of the utmost value.

Inside the fort is a well which gives a good supply of water, but, worked as it is with a windlass and bucket, the process of getting water for a large number of people is tedious in the extreme. It became necessary, therefore, to draw water from the springs which, lying about fifty yards from the fort, afford the usual supply in peaceful times. It was with great difficulty that the carriers could be induced, even under an armed escort, to venture beyond the precincts of the fort; but after the first attempt, and when it was found that the rebels offered no resistance, they readily fell in for the work at the appointed times. Had we been unable to use this water supply, great indeed would have been the sufferings of the refugees, for the fort well could not possibly have supplied the wants of all. It was one of our fears that the rebels would find a way of either poisoning or polluting the springs, but fortunately for us this never seemed to strike them, and throughout the siege water in any quantity was readily obtainable.

The day wore on. Immediate anxiety had been dispelled when we found that the rebels did not intend to molest us, but weary in body and mind we were glad when it came to an end. The night was not to be without excitement. Heavy clouds were seen to be gathering in the distance, denoting that a tornado was imminent. In the stillness of the night it broke upon the town with all its fury. First a hurricane of wind rushing through the forest trees, sweeping everything before it in its mad career, and then a heavy, blinding, drenching rain.

The refugees, poor things! without any shelter, made a greater noise than ever, and tried, as best they could, to protect themselves against the elements. Fortunately for them the tornado did not last long; but they were in a sad plight, and to our consternation they lighted fires, hoping thereby to dry themselves and their belongings. These fires apparently attracted the rebels, for an alarm was given by one of our sentries that they were coming. All those in the fort were up and doing in a moment. Officers were hurrying about and ·

Hemmed in by Savage Hordes

everyone on the *qui vive;* but fortunately it turned out to be only an alarm, and in about an hour's time all was quiet again. The rebels, I am sure, meant an attack; but we were on the move sooner than they expected, and so prevented it. There was a dear old Hausa sentry on the veranda near to my bedroom who regarded me as his special charge. On this occasion, and on others when my curiosity prompted me to go on the veranda to see what was happening, this old man would push me back, saying, in very broken English, "Ashanti man come. No come out."

We had an alarm again the next night; this time a more serious one, for shots were exchanged, and the firing was taken up all down the line drawn round the refugees for their protection. The day had been much the same as the preceding one, only more dreary and dispiriting for us, if that were possible. The refugees were allowed to throw up shelters of such a height as not to inter-fere with the firing of the guns from the fort, should it be necessary to use them. It was wonderful how soon these shelters were erected—in about a couple of hours a complete village was built up. Stout forked sticks or poles were stuck into the ground, with cross-pieces resting in the forks; a roof was manufactured out of similar sticks, and over all were lashed cloths and skins of all descriptions. The more courageous ventured to go as far as the nearest huts, and taking off the thatched roofing staggered back with it. There was not much to take, for the rebels had burnt down most of the huts. The Ashantis seemed always to be very busy, but it was considered best to leave them alone until the garrison had been strengthened by the arrival of the Hausas from Lagos, who were known to be on their way up. We had fortunately been able to have authentic news of their movements, and were anxiously expecting them that Saturday. Towards evening, however, it was vaguely rumoured that they had been severely attacked near the River Ordah, and had been compelled to laager for the night.

At noon the rebels fired the prison buildings, which were some 300 yards away from the fort. They were built of swish, but the thatched roofing to the huts burnt furiously. Fortunately the stockade around the buildings was not injured, and later when we had been reinforced it was occupied by one of our outposts. The prisoners had been released on Wednesday, as soon as it was found necessary to concentrate on the fort.

Hemmed in by Savage Hordes

Many of them went over to the rebels, while others stayed with us, and were doing good work as scavengers and so forth. While the prison was burning the wind was blowing in the direction of the fort, and carrying towards us not only sparks, but also small pieces of burning thatch, and I feared every moment that the woodwork of the fort would ignite. This work of destruction was apparently to have been followed by the burning of the hospital and medical officers' bungalow, but as these were somewhat closer to the fort it was possible to protect them. Arrangements were made accordingly, and as soon as the rebels appeared they were cleared out.

CHAPTER VIII

SUCCESS AND REINFORCEMENT

THE non-arrival of the Lagos Hausas and the uncertainty as to their fate were very depressing, and later, when after darkness had closed in upon us it was found that the rebels had managed to creep up to the hospital out-buildings and set fire to them, my spirits fell to zero.

Sunday the 29th April was to be a notable day. We were all early astir, and so apparently were the rebels, for we could see them moving about in ones and twos in all directions—some more venturous than others even getting into the hospital, and as we thought preparing it for destruction by throwing kerosene oil about to stimulate the flames. The general feeling was that the Lagos Hausas would make a determined attempt to push on and get into Kumassi, and it was decided to do everything possible to harass the rebels and induce them to attack us, so as to draw off as many of them as possible from the approaching column. All the morning, therefore, they were sniped, worried, and kept on the move. I could watch the proceedings from the veranda of our quarters, and it was really amusing to see the Ashantis ducking as the shots whizzed past them, and then taking to their heels and making for cover. Our tactics were successful, for at 12.30 p.m. they commenced an attack upon us.

They had during the night carefully loopholed the huts in the Hausa cantonments which faced towards the fort, and from these they opened a terrific fusillade, which was, however, harmless, as the range was too long for their guns. Our only reply was to send a few shells into their position from the 7-pounder gun in the bastion of the fort facing it. The Hausas were under arms and ready for the next move. This was soon to come, for the rebels, finding that the bursting shells rendered their position untenable, instead of retiring, swarmed out into the open and advanced upon the fort.

Then commenced a fight which I was obliged to witness, and which, although at first terrifying, became at last exciting and engrossing. Cowering down under the walls of the fort were the refugees, and around them were the Hausas ready for the attack. In the fort were the gunners standing to their guns, which everywhere were prepared for action. The advance of the rebels was met by a terrific fire from the Maxims in the fort, which I knew was effective, as I could see them dropping. But nothing daunted on they came, and now the fire was taken up by the Hausas. The din was very great, and so close to the fort was the fighting that the slugs from the rebels' guns fell in the fort yard, and a brass lamp which was standing on the floor of the veranda was hit and dented while I was standing quite close to it. At this moment one of the medical officers rushed in to request me to go inside, as my white dress was as good as a target, and some of the rebels had arms of precision.

The rebels were now falling fast, and the Hausas were pressing them back. It became almost a hand-to-hand fight, and the guns in the fort had to cease fire. At last a cheer proclaimed that the enemy were retiring. Then it was that our loyal natives, some two hundred of whom we had managed to arm, came into play, and did good service under the Governor's private secretary, Captain Armitage, who on this occasion and later controlled and led them. Everywhere were signs of victory. The rebels had been defeated, and joy was once more aglow on every face. I watched the advance of the loyal natives. At their head were their chiefs, prominent amongst whom was the King of Aguna, dressed in his fetish war coat. It was a handsome barbaric vestment in the form of a jumper, not unlike the "jibba" worn by the Arabs of the Soudan, and was hung back and front with fetish charms made from snake and other skins, or bits of coloured cloths. He also wore a pair of thick leather boots, and where these ended his black legs began and continued, until they met well above the knee a short trouser of coloured cotton. He also wore a fierce-looking head-dress, and carried war charms made up chiefly of elephant tails. Proudly and well did he bear himself, and when the fight was over he was triumphantly carried back on the shoulders of two of his warriors to the fort, outside of which he met with a great ovation from his "ladies," who flocked round him, pressing forward to shake his hand, and doubtless —if one could have understood the clatter and chatter—to congratulate him upon the victory of the day.

The fight was over and we had won. Everywhere the rebels had been repulsed with loss. Our losses were comparatively slight, namely, one killed and three wounded, while the casualties of the enemy had been very severe. Many of their dead they succeeded in taking away with them, but the next day we buried more than a hundred and thirty bodies. Throughout the engagement the Hausas fought with great steadiness, and were ably assisted by the loyal natives; together they showed the rebels that it was useless to attack the fort. Captain Middlemist was too ill to take the command, which consequently devolved upon Captain G. Marshall, Royal West Kent Regiment, and well must he have handled the men and done his work. When the engagement was over three cheers were given for the Queen, and then, poor fellow! he succumbed, and was brought into our quarters half delirious. He had been overcome with the heat of the sun and the hard exacting work which the engagement demanded, but he pulled through all right, and was well again the next day.

Our victory meant much for us, for not only had we driven the rebels out of Kumassi and across the swamps, but we were enabled to secure large supplies of food and warlike stores which in their flight they had left behind. It was clear from the quantities of these that fell into our hands that the rebels had made up their minds to stay, and had not contemplated defeat and flight. The

THE FORT, KUMASSI

faces of the refugees brightened with joy at the changed aspect of affairs, and it was difficult to believe that they were the same beings who in the morning had cowered under the fort with troubled and anxious looks.

Once more our thoughts reverted to the Lagos Hausas. Were they likely to reach Kumassi that day? Had our engagement drawn off the rebels and helped them? These were the questions which we asked each other. The afternoon wore on, and as each hour passed we began to fear some disaster might have overtaken them. Four o'clock came, five o'clock, and still no sign of them. The excitement of our own victory was now lost sight of in anxiety as to where the Lagos Hausas could be. I remember looking at a small bee clock on the table as I walked up and down the room, and saying to myself that if six o'clock came without bringing them, the worst must be feared. But before half-past five firing was heard on the Cape Coast road, and we knew that they could not be very far away. We sent a force down the road to meet them, and just before six o'clock a cry was raised that the Hausas were coming, and sure enough within ten minutes they appeared round the bend of the road. What a joyful sight

Success and Reinforcement

it was to see this reinforcement, and to them the scene which met their gaze must have been memorable: the silent fort standing out grim and stately in the gloaming, the little village which had sprung up under its walls, and the crowds of people who lined the road to the gates, anxious to catch a glimpse of the men who had pushed their way up from the coast.

It was not long before we heard of the terrible time they had gone through. The brave officers were all wounded, one of them very severely. They had had nothing to eat or drink since early morning, but we soon relieved their wants, and eagerly listened to their tales of woe and adventure. The men were marched at once into the fort, and so tired were they that after hasty refreshment they just threw themselves down and slept. The force which had arrived was commanded by Captain J. G. O. Aplin, C.M.G., Inspector-General of Lagos Constabulary, and I cannot, I think, do better than quote the account of the fighting, which, upon his return to England, he gave to Reuter's representative who interviewed him. It is as follows :—

"On the march up we burnt a number of deserted villages in the Ashanti country, but met no natives. The first heavy fighting took place at a

Success and Reinforcement

village called Esiago, when we were attacked on
either flank by a very large force of the enemy,
who occupied the trees on either side of the track,
and from the branches poured down a withering
fire upon the column. Our advance guard had
been allowed to pass; there was not a sign of a
native anywhere, and the road was as still as death
when the main column was suddenly attacked. A
halt was called, and the men were formed up two
deep, kneeling, and facing the bush in opposite
directions.

"We were soon amid a perfect rain of slugs, and
pieces of telegraph line which the Ashantis had
cut into lengths and twisted in various shapes, but
we could not see a soul, as the enemy after firing
slid down the trunks of the trees into the jungle.
Soon the advance guard was also attacked, and the
whole column was gradually enveloped. Captain
Cochrane, who was commanding the advance guard
and firing the Maxim, was hit in the shoulder, but
refused to leave his post until he became faint from
loss of blood, and Dr. Macfarlane, while tending
him, was also wounded. At this juncture the
machine guns became overheated, and jammed, and
had to be put out of action; and the opposition
was so great that it took us two hours to fight
our way to the village less than half a mile distant.
In addition to Captain Cochrane and Dr. Macfarlane, I was slightly wounded by a bullet which
passed through the brim of my helmet, grazed the

cheek, and passed through my orderly's leg, after striking my breast. The enemy were temporarily driven off, but as we advanced they returned to the attack, and before their village was occupied they had attacked us four times. Eventually the place was shelled, and then the advance guard charged with fixed bayonets. Next morning the village was burnt to the ground.

"On reaching the Ordah River, where the Ashantis made their great stand of 1872, we met with desperate resistance from a force of the enemy estimated at four thousand. The action commenced soon after crossing the river, at about 11 a.m., and lasted without intermission until five in the evening, our position at one time being very critical. As before, there was at first no sign of the enemy beyond an occasional suspicious movement of the jungle grass. Suddenly a turn in the track brought to view a formidable stockade extending in horseshoe shape. Then we saw the Ashantis looking over the top and peering between the logs forming the stockade.

"The track was so narrow that we had no front for firing, yet the whole path was swept by the enemy's guns. We became so hard pressed that I sent back for Captain Read to bring up half the rearguard. Orders were given to outflank the stockade, and Captain Cochrane and thirty Hausas crept away into the bush with this object. Again our Maxim jammed, and the 7 - pounder was brought up into line ; but soon we became short of ammunition, and as a last resort the 7-pounder was loaded with gravel and stones from the track. At the same time orders were given to fix bayonets, but the men were so done up, and the guns were so hot from continued firing, that a charge seemed almost out of the question.

"At this critical moment three volleys announced that Captain Cochrane had enfiladed the stockade, and the Ashanti fire slackened. The charge was ordered, but for a moment the worn-out troops hesitated, when a native officer, waving his sword and addressing his men in Hausa, adjured them in God's name to charge. They rose as one man, almost knocking me over in their enthusiasm, and charged the stockade. Captain Read and his men also charged in face of a terrific fire, and got to within five yards of the stockade, but almost every one of his men were hit, and he himself was wounded in five places. His party had to retire, and just as they got back to the main column Captain Read was again hit in the head. Just before this Lieutenant Ralph had been twice wounded, every one of the officers of the force having thus been hit. After taking this stockade, the column advanced at the double into Coomassie."

Brought in by the Lagos Hausas was a Government officer who had been terribly knocked about

Success and Reinforcement

by the rebels. This officer, Mr. Branch, was in the telegraph department, and was engaged in superintending the maintenance of telegraphic communication between Kumassi and Cape Coast. When we came up we had found him at Prahsu, but after the rising, when the telegraph wires were being cut, he had come on to Kwisa, and eventually had made his way to Esumeja. Up to this point he had managed to keep the wire in working order to Cape Coast, but there was no communication with Kumassi.

On the 18th or 19th April the Acting Resident arrived at Esumeja on his way to the coast, and Mr. Branch gathering from a conversation with him that there was really nothing to fear, and that anyone could travel without molestation, started off full of zeal to put the line right to Kumassi. Half-way up his peaceful party was attacked. One of his hammock-men was shot, and his carriers threw down their loads and bolted. Fortunately for him he had taken off his helmet and placed it at the foot of his hammock, and the rebels thinking that his head must be under it directed their guns at it. It was riddled by the slugs. Jumping out of his hammock he was making for the bush, but was caught and unmercifully beaten about the legs

Success and Reinforcement

and feet; he managed, however, to make good his escape, his life being saved by his dog. The poor little beast, following his master as he ran, was fired upon and wounded, and went off yelping into the bush in a different direction. The Ashantis not knowing this pursued the dog, and so its master eluded them. Night came on and found him wandering back towards Esumeja, fearful of meeting natives at every turn of his path. As daylight came he managed to find the main road, but hardly had he emerged into it when he heard voices drawing nearer and nearer. He threw himself down at the side of the road hoping to be hidden, and could hear the natives as they came along. His agony of mind, he said, was terrible, for the fear of torture was before him. At last they came up to his hiding-place and discovered him. But to his joy he found from the signs they made that they were friends.

His carriers and servant on the previous day had rushed back to the nearest village, and told the chief what had happened. The friendly Kokofu chief instantly sent out a rescue party to bring him in dead or alive. They had searched all night, and at last came upon him, and carried him back to Esumeja, where he remained until the arrival of the Lagos Hausas on the 27th of April. They then brought him on to receive medical treatment and comforts at Kumassi, never thinking what a struggle lay before them to reach the town. It was a pitiful sight to see him helped from his hammock into the fort, hardly able to put his feet to the ground so painful and swollen were they.

However, a few days' rest and attention did wonders for him, and he was soon able to take his share of work with the other Europeans in the fort, and those were busy days for all.

Our success on Sunday had so changed the complexion of affairs that we were able to retire to rest, feeling hopeful and far more cheerful as to our position. It was a day to be remembered, for it had given us victory over the rebels, food for the Hausas and others, and welcome reinforcements.

With the morning I was to learn that things were not quite as I had pictured them. The Lagos Hausas had not brought with them the supply of rice and ammunition which had been ordered up. The desertion of carriers had compelled them to leave the rice behind at Prahsu, and the greater part of the ammunition had been

Success and Reinforcement

expended in their fierce encounters with the rebels. Food and ammunition were what we wanted, for now we had two hundred and fifty additional men to feed from our comparatively slender stores, to which practically no addition had been made.

CHAPTER IX

REBELS CHANGE THEIR TACTICS

DURING the days immediately following the arrival of the Lagos Hausas it was seen that the rebels, baffled in their intention of storming and taking the fort, had changed their tactics, and had determined to prevent our getting away. We were to be starved out, and for that purpose they took steps to prevent the success of our foraging parties, and by effectually blocking the roads to stop all communication with the fort. A more effectual siege had in fact commenced.

The extent of our food supply stored in the fort was of course well known to the Governor, but this supply was for the men composing the garrison, and we found ourselves with loyal native kings and chiefs and their armed and unarmed followers, numbering at least five hundred, as well as an equal number of Government carriers, and nearly three thousand refugees. How was this multitude to be fed until relief came, and with it

MAJOR A. MORRIS, D.S.O.
ROYAL IRISH REGIMENT

Face page 144

supplies of food and warlike stores? This had now become the burning question. The Mohammedan butchers had a few head of cattle which, when they had fled from their settlement on the outskirts of Kumassi, they had brought with them, and there were four Government cows. The slaughter of these animals was carefully restricted, and as a matter of fact the last was killed on the 27th May. Poultry, eggs, and fruit were not to be had for love or money, the refugees who were fortunate enough to possess them very wisely refusing to part with them, and keeping them for their own use. One of the cows was such a very pretty animal, and very tame. It was held in much affection, having been in Kumassi almost as long as the Union Jack. Many were the tales and adventures related about this animal, and as they had always ended happily we took comfort in this thought, saying that relief would surely arrive before the fatal day came when the cow must be killed. But alas! fate ruled otherwise, for the time came when all others had been slaughtered, and so the historic cow found its way on to several tables, but not on to mine, for I preferred to eat the ration of tinned corned beef rather than set aside sentiment. This was the last fresh meat available until June 25th, when we had some at Nkwanta.

Serving out the rations every morning to the Hausas and others entitled to them was a great business, and one that had to be very closely watched and attended, for to take unobserved an extra tin of biscuits or corned beef, or even one biscuit, was thought no robbery, but rather a clever trick. The chances of such pilfering were however few, owing to the excellent supervision of Dr. Tweedly and Mr. Grundy, mining engineer, whose duty it was to control the distribution. The ration was truly luxurious fare! At first a few tins of "Maconachie rations" were available, and afterwards an article of food known as corned beef. Then, too, there were biscuits that even at this distance of time make one shudder to think of. The best description of them is perhaps to style them "puppy biscuits." They were almost unnegotiable even to those endowed by nature with good teeth, but a hopeless case to others who were not so fortunate. Now these delicacies had attained to the age of four years in a tropical climate, and in order to form a correct idea of how we existed during all the latter weeks of the siege, and to complete the picture of our daily ration, which consisted of one pound of tinned meat and one biscuit, this must be remembered, because the meat ration, upon the tin being opened, was often found to be enriched by a coating of green mould, and the biscuit had, not unfrequently, to be carefully guarded lest it should be walked off with by the ubiquitous weevil. Yet we were thankful enough for this food, such as it was, and grateful that the Government had had the foresight to place it in the store-rooms of the fort.

The garrison having been strengthened by the arrival of the Lagos Hausas, it was found possible to reoccupy the cantonments and other buildings which we had regained from the rebels. The refugees were at the same time required to leave the vicinity of the fort and live in huts in those parts of Kumassi which could be guarded by our troops, and were thus considered safe. What a relief it was when this seething mass of humanity moved away! The last few days had been very trying. Windows had to be kept closed because of the horrible smells that the little breeze there was wafted in. The air seemed stifling, and the scenes which met the gaze on all sides were not always agreeable. Then, again, the noise that had never ceased from the first moment was growing wearisome. One of the officers, Captain Middle-mist, was seriously ill, and we tried to make the vast crowd under his window cease their chatter and shouting, for rest was essential to him; but all our pleadings were in vain, the noise remained incessant. He died, to our great regret, on Sunday, May 6th, and was buried under a clump of trees close to the fort, a pretty spot looking out towards the forest on the west. There he found his last resting-place, leaving us to mourn his loss, for he was a brave, true-hearted soldier, loving his work, and bringing all his energy to bear upon it. It was a sad day for all of us.

It will not be out of place here to relate the faithfulness of his native servant. He was a "boy" from the Northern Territories, and his name was Mounchi. He was very awkward and silly in the sick-room, and I am afraid was often, by myself and others, abused for the stupidity that he really could not help, but he was at hand whenever anything was wanted, and at night never left his master's room. His grief was very great when the end came, and the morning after the funeral Mounchi was found lying on the grave of his master sobbing bitterly. He was taken by one of the other officers as his servant, and, strange to say, Mounchi's powers as a "rough diamond" nurse were once again called into requisition, for his new master was taken seriously ill with fever, but partly owing to Mounchi's experience he was nursed safely through it.

The food question was becoming daily more serious. The refugees had still a small quantity left from the supply which they had brought with them on April 23rd, and were in these days able to get a limited amount by digging the ground for edible roots, but as time went on it was heart-rending to see the same ground turned over and over again on the off-chance that even one root had escaped observation in previous searches. If only the food ordered by the Governor to be sent from the coast could have been brought in by the Lagos Hausas as we had hoped it would be!

On the 18th of May I went out of the fort for the first time since the commencement of the siege, and saw Kumassi in its new guise. The broad street leading up to the cantonments was alive with people, and a picturesque scene it was. As one rounded the corner of the fort wall both sides of the street came into view, bright with the coloured cloths of men and women busy about their every-day occupations, without a thought of their recent panic and misery, and apparently fully trusting those who were in authority. Fires were lighted in front of many of the low-roofed shelter huts they had been allowed to build, and women were pounding foo-foo and grinding corn, making ready for the scanty evening meal of the men. Those whose trade had been that of pedlars had formed a bazaar, or market, on either side of the road, and all their stock-in-trade was displayed to purchasers. The Mohammedans in their quaint and picturesque robes and turbans were busy at leather work and various kinds of stitching and embroidery, and the scene, except for the smallness of the huts and their close proximity to each other, would have appeared to a stranger a peaceful and contented one. We spoke to several as we passed along, and made a few purchases to encourage the sellers. I bought also three coloured glass bracelets as mementoes of this curious scene, but these were unfortunately lost with many more things on our march to the coast.

Then we went on to the cantonments, and saw what the rebels had been so busy about during their three days' residence there. They had most cleverly and cunningly not only loopholed the huts facing the fort and the road, but also made openings in the inner party-walls large enough to enable them to run from one to the other in safety and under shelter. It was a very ingenious piece of work, and showed us that we had no despicable enemy to contend with. I was also taken to see the trenches which had been thrown up by our men at all points of vantage. They were manned day and night, and a sharp look-out was kept against attack.

Next I had to inspect a stockade which had been erected by our troops across the road not far from the Basel Mission House. This was the limit of safety on the Bantama road, and although there was a picket posted further on, I was not allowed to go beyond the stockade. Our next visit was to the prison, which had been fortified and turned into barracks for some of the Hausas, and there we brought our walk to an end by looking at the bullet marks on several houses made by our guns during our two great fights in Kumassi. Several of the iron telegraph poles along the roads and in the line of fire had holes right through them, and everywhere were signs of battle, or of wanton destruction by the rebels.

Every evening after this, between five and six o'clock, I used to take this one walk of about a quarter of a mile. How tired I was of it at last, and then as time went on what terrible sights met the eye! Starving and wan faces turned to us, silently asking for the pity and help that we were powerless to render. Money was all we had to give, and give it we did, hoping that the recipient might with it be able to buy a small quantity of food, and thus prolong his waning life. The rebels kept a close watch on all our movements, and had so hedged us in that it was well-nigh impossible for the refugees to elude their vigilance and find food in the neighbouring plantations. Occasionally fortune would favour the brave, and those who were courageous enough to go beyond the known zone of safety would return with a small supply of plantains, which they would sell at exorbitant prices. More often than not the brave foodseeker would never return, having failed to evade the rebel pickets, or would be brought in by his comrades wounded and bleeding.

On the 2nd of May a reconnaissance was made along the road leading to the Northern Territories, in order to see what the strength of the rebels was in that direction, and whether there was any possibility of securing food. It was found that a very strong stockade had been placed across the road close to the house of the Wesleyan Mission, the residence of the native pastor, who before the Governor's arrival in Kumassi had left for the coast. The loyal natives were on this occasion employed under Captain Armitage, and fought well, their casualties being one killed and thirty wounded; three Hausas were also wounded. Two days afterwards the Wesleyan Mission Station was burnt to the ground, and the rebels destroyed their stockade, reconstructing it further back in the bush.

On the 8th, 9th, and 10th of May armed forces were sent out to assist the native levies in obtaining food, but on each occasion found the rebels in such strength as to preclude all chance of getting it, except by a severe engagement, which was considered unadvisable, as it was necessary to husband our stock of ammunition in case of attack, or for fighting our way out if no relief arrived.

Night after night I was terrified by the noise of drumming in the rebel camps. At times I could hear in the stillness the weird sound of a horn which blown in one camp would be answered in the next, and thus echoed from camp to camp until the sound died away in the distance. The loyal kings and chiefs would tell us that the drums were beating out exultation and defiance, and with anxious faces would beg the Governor to hurry up troops to our aid. But how could this be done? An Intelligence Department had been organised, and spies were sent out daily, who brought in their reports, sometimes good and sometimes the reverse, while more often than not it was clear they had been manufactured. The good news was always believed, and the day was brighter and happier for it. The bad news we always sought to minimise. Not a line of any kind, not an authentic scrap of news, reached us from the outside world from the 29th April, the day on which the Lagos Hausas arrived at Kumassi, until the 8th July. Throughout we knew nothing of a relief column. Every day we hoped for news of it, but neither news nor column arrived, and each day we had to glean such comfort as we could from the vague, meagre, and uncertain reports brought to us by our people.

I remember one day, after a long hiatus of even native rumours, we were taking our evening stroll, when one of the chiefs, who was indefatigable in sending out his people to gather news, came rushing up to the Governor, and in his best English said that a woman who had been taken prisoner by the rebels had escaped, and had brought news of a relief column. We hurried back to the fort, sending

the chief to bring the woman at once, so that we might hear her joyful tidings. An interpreter came with the party, but what was he saying? Instead of good news it was to the effect that disaster had overtaken a force on its way to us—that, in fact, it had been repulsed with heavy loss. We could not believe it, and said that the woman had invented the story. Alas! as we afterwards learnt, it was only too true. That evening we had a few officers to a "ration" dinner. Everyone avoided the subject uppermost in his mind, and although each was wondering if the others had heard the dismal rumour, no one wished to be the first to spread it. So the evening passed with a greater show of gaiety than usual, and with a cheerfulness that hid heavy hearts.

CHAPTER X

FRIENDS FROM THE NORTH

ON the 11th of May the loyal kings notified
that they would like to open negotiations
with the rebel chiefs in the hope of staying further
hostilities, and so preventing Ashanti being laid
waste by the Queen's troops when they should
come up. Permission was given, and the messengers
from the kings left the fort at 6 p.m. For four
days negotiations proceeded, during which, the
vigilance of the rebels having been somewhat
relaxed, the refugees found themselves able to
obtain a little food from the plantations beyond
Bantama. Presents of loads of plantains were also
sent to the loyal kings, with a message from the
rebel chiefs that they did not want them to suffer,
that they were fighting against the white men who
had taken their country, and not against their own
people. In the end the negotiations proved futile,
as was expected, but they had at least done some
good in enabling our people to secure some provisions.

Friends from the North

In the meantime reports had been brought in from spies that troops from the Northern Territories were nearing Kumassi, and that several engagements had been fought between them and the rebels. It was also rumoured that the Adansis and the N'Koranzas to the north had risen against us. The rising of the Adansis, if true, as it turned out to be, meant trouble and difficulty to the troops coming up to relieve us, while that of the N'Koranzas, which proved to be incorrect in the main, meant fighting for the troops from the Northern Territories, because in order to reach Kumassi they had to pass through the country of the N'Koranza tribe.

On the morning of the 15th of May word came in that Hausas from the Northern Territories were within a couple of hours of us. Great was our excitement, but the two hours passed and they did not come. We were by this time grown accustomed to disappointment, and so we regarded the rumour as one to be set down as worthless. However, about 3.30 p.m. there was a terrific hubbub all round the fort, and we rushed out on to the veranda to see what was the matter. Hundreds of people were streaming towards the Northern Territories road, and on asking what it was we

were told that large loads of food were being
brought in. In a very few minutes we saw for
ourselves what the commotion was all about. The
joyful sight greeted us of Major Morris bringing
in his troops from the Northern Territories. Such
a fine body of men they were, all of them wearing
the picturesque, multi-coloured straw hats which
are used in the Northern Territories, as the country
there is open and the sun heat very great. Some
of the officers were on ponies, and a gay cavalcade
it looked as it advanced up the road. The g et-
ings on all sides were hearty—officers, Hausas, and
carriers all meeting friends and acquaintances. The
contrast between their healthy faces and our poor
emaciated ones was very severe. They had made
a record march, but not without some severe fighting. Major Morris himself had been wounded
shortly before reaching Kumassi while leading his
men to charge a stockade, and was suffering great
pain when he arrived at the fort. An account of
the march given by one of his officers to Reuter's
representative is interesting reading. It runs as
follows :—

"On April 18th the first reports reached the
British garrison at Gambaga of trouble with the
Ashantis, and immediately Major A. Morris, D.S.O.,

the Commissioner of the Northern Territories, who was in command at headquarters, commenced preparations to march to Kumassi, 340 miles to the south. In three days everything was in readiness, and the force, consisting of 4 officers, 170 Hausas of all ranks, a 7-pounder gun, and a Maxim, set out for the south, with Major Morris in command. In addition to this force, there was a troop of Moshi cavalry, a native volunteer force, which had been raised by Major Morris, and had been successfully employed in the Northern Territories against unfriendly tribes. During the march to Kumassi the weather was very trying—extremely hot in the daytime, with torrential rains at night. The force marched along the narrow track in single file, the column being about a mile in length.

"Six days after we had left headquarters, urgent despatches were received from the Governor, requesting Major Morris to proceed to his assistance at once. Rushing ahead with all speed, the force reached Kintampo, 238 miles from our starting-place, and 100 from Kumassi, in 13 days, really a splendid performance, averaging 17 miles a day. A halt of two days was necessary at Kintampo to concentrate the force, and advantage was taken of this stop to send messages to the powerful N'Koranzas, with the hope of persuading them to remain loyal. This Major Morris succeeded in accomplishing.

"At half-past six on the morning of May 9th

the reinforced column, which now consisted of 7 white officers and 230 non-commissioned officers and men, with machine guns, and 82 native levies, under Major Morris, left Kintampo for Kumassi. During the first twenty-four hours nothing of any importance occurred, but much anxiety was felt as to whether the N'Koranzas, whose town we were rapidly approaching, would prove loyal. The chief, who had previously been friendly to us, had been seized by the Ashantis and compelled to swear that he would fight the British; but his sister, the Princess, resolutely refused to abandon her ancient loyalty. She would probably have been forced to side with the Ashantis had we not reached the town in the nick of time, thus supporting the Princess, and enabling the King to defy the Ashantis. The Princess and her followers met us outside the town with great rejoicing.

"Major Morris, immediately after our arrival, ordered a big palaver, in which he expressed his pleasure at the loyalty of the Princess, who was overjoyed when told that the town would not be burnt.

"The loyalty of this great people being secured, the march was resumed, and we penetrated into the thick of the enemy's country. The deserted village of N'Quanta was burnt, and soon we reached a broad river, where scouts exchanged shots with the enemy, who retired rapidly. Two hours later we encountered their main body in ambush in the grass outside the large town of Sekedumassi. A galling fire was opened upon our advance guard, but on our machine gun coming into action the enemy bolted. Our march had been so rapid that the Ashantis, who lost heavily, were surprised. Our casualties were only three wounded. We at once occupied the town, where we were glad to find a large quantity of half-cooked meat, and encamped for the night after forming square around the place.

"The night passed quietly, and early next morning a flying column was despatched to destroy the adjacent unfriendly town of Frantee. This having been accomplished, the column returned to Sekedumassi, the destruction of which place was then completed. In this town we found a large fetish grove, with the remains of very recent human sacrifices. The stench was awful, the sacrificial receptacles under the great trees containing fresh human blood and portions of mutilated bodies.

"An area of deserted country was now crossed, and on the following day two more villages were burnt to the ground without opposition. In one of these villages we found a woman, who said that all the warriors had congregated two hours from Kumassi in order to oppose our advance.

"Rapidly the position became more threatening, and on May 14th, two hours after we had destroyed one of the enemy's towns, our native levies became heavily engaged, having walked straight into an ambush. They fell back on our advance columns, and after heavy firing, in which we had twelve casualties, the Ashantis were driven off. The ambush had been very cleverly planned behind a great tree.

"During the remainder of that day we entered and burnt three more villages. We found the country deserted, the Ashantis having evidently, in view of our unexpectedly rapid march, fallen back for the purpose of concentrating near the capital.

"May 15th, the date of our arrival at Kumassi, was a day of incessant fighting, in the course of which Major Morris was severely wounded in the groin while leading an attack. The previous night the force encamped at Braman, in the midst of a dense plantain farm, and as an extra precaution all sentries were doubled. Early on the morning of the 15th scouts brought in word that a strong Ashanti ambush had been prepared in front of us, and shortly afterwards we saw an ugly stockade right across the road. The 7-pounder was at once brought into action to draw the enemy's fire, and in a few minutes the Ashantis replied with volleys from all directions. In about an hour the fusillade ceased, except from behind the stockade, which Major Morris decided must be rushed without delay. The · charge was ordered, Major Morris and Captain Maguire running in front of their men. The former had not proceeded twenty yards before he was badly wounded, and fell in the road. The stockade was eventually taken with the loss of Major Morris and fifteen Hausas wounded, and at three o'clock the same afternoon Kumassi was reached, Major Morris continuing to direct the operations from his hammock, although in intense pain, with intervals of unconsciousness.

"The first stockade taken, the advance was rapidly continued to prevent the enemy from re-forming. A second stockade was encountered eight hundred yards to the rear, six feet high, on which even the 7-pounder had no effect, and scarcely had this been scaled before a third stockade was discovered. Our rapid advance had, however, entirely disconcerted the enemy, who had evidently prepared to oppose us strongly at this point. Kumassi was still some twelve miles distant. We continued our advance until we reached one of the investing stockades round the capital. To our great surprise this particular one was not held at the moment of our arrival, and we entered Kumassi without further opposition. During the day's fighting we had killed several hundred Ashantis, including a number of important chiefs.

"At 3 p.m. on May the 15th, to our great relief, we caught sight of the fort at Kumassi, and saw that the Union Jack was still flying from the flagstaff. A few minutes later Major Morris was receiving the congratulations of the besieged garrison on his splendid march from the north.

Friends from the North

"We found the town was invested on every side. For a radius of a mile round the fort the Ashantis had erected very strong stockades, each communicating with the other by a path, so that every point could be quickly reinforced. Each stockade faced our fort, was about six feet in height, and loopholed at the top. Behind these obstacles, which were made of great baulks of timber, the enemy were encamped. Having unsuccessfully attacked the fort already, the Ashantis now acted on the defensive rather than the offensive, so that within the radius of a mile the garrison were able to move about. Within this inclosure were a number of other buildings beside the fort. Three hundred yards distant were the Hausa lines, which were occupied and connected by entrenchments with the jail, in which there was also a Hausa garrison. All the other buildings outside the fort were deserted, but within musketry range ; the loyal native inhabitants were encamped in huts, while in the fort were the Governor and Lady Hodgson, three Basel missionaries and their wives, some mining engineers, and about half a dozen officers, the remainder being with their men in the Hausa lines."

ASHANTI FETISH TEMPLE

Face page 168

CHAPTER XI

BRAVE HEARTS AND TRUE

THE arrival of Major Morris seemed to take
a load off our minds. He was so cheery,
confident, and resourceful, and seemed always able
to raise the spirits of the faint-hearted. We were
now able to reoccupy a further part of Kumassi
known as Asafu, the Gambaga Hausas as they
were styled making it their barracks. The large
loads of food before mentioned as seen coming
in did not in reality exist, but the Gambagas
brought in a sufficient supply to last them about
a week. This did not help us and the refugees,
and, as regards food, we were not only no better
off than before, but worse, for now rations had
to be provided for the new arrivals, and for the
carriers and Mohammedan levies who had accompanied them. They, however, brought ammunition, and this was something, for it meant that
we might be able to push home an attack, and
thus secure the food we wanted.

Brave Hearts and True

Major Morris, in command of the forces, which together numbered 750 of all ranks, determined to ascertain the strength of the rebels on the eastern side of the town. Accordingly, on the 20th May, a reconnaissance in force was made, the enemy being attacked in two places simultaneously. At both points the rebels were found to be in overwhelming numbers. The reconnaissance was useful, as it gave us a knowledge of the enemy's strength, and a further insight into the construction and disposition of the stockades, and told us what had before only been surmised—that the 7-pounder gun was practically useless against them, splendidly constructed as they were of huge trees and logs, loopholed, and in many cases provided with head-shelter. We also learnt from this reconnaissance that the rebels had provided themselves with shelter-pits, so as to enable them to take cover when shelled by our guns.

I think this morning's fight was the most terrifying of any that had taken place. Nothing of it was visible from the fort. All the officers were on duty, and the place seemed to be deserted. The wives of the refugees were doing a slow funeral dance up and down the road, and at the same time chaunting a mournful dirge, their faces and bodies daubed with fetish signs in white paint. In their hands they carried small branches of leaves, which they waved in unison. They were calling upon their gods. to give victory to their husbands and friends. This was nerve-shaking enough, but nothing to what followed when the first firing commenced : it was comparatively close at hand, and the noise was incessant. It was difficult to distinguish our fire from that of the rebels, their guns being so plentiful as to sound like a never-ceasing Maxim. The fort resounded with the echoes, and news from the scene of the fight was anxiously awaited.

Presently the wounded began to be carried past to the hospital. I saw a hammock coming with a white officer in it, and as it passed by I recognised Captain Leggett. It was saturated with blood, and he looked so pained and white that I could not restrain my pent-up feelings any longer, but gave way to tears, for I thought he must be dead. He had been in my room only an hour before confident that all would go well, and that the Maxim gun he was to work would not fail to play havoc amongst the rebels. It was a great relief to hear, as I soon did, that he was not killed, but only very severely wounded.

Brave Hearts and True

While working the Maxim gun he had been shot, and owing to the unevenness of the ground he and the gun had rolled over together. While righting the gun he received his second and severer wound. I went to see him later, and found him, although in great pain and disgusted at being laid by for a time, as cheery as usual, and full of courage. Our casualties on this occasion amounted to twenty-nine wounded, of whom two subsequently died.

On the 20th May, Opoku Mensa, the senior member of the Native Committee, died in the fort of pneumonia. He had throughout his illness been carefully looked after, but he was a very old man, and, broken in mind and body, succumbed. It was strange how soon his death became known, for the next day we could hear the rebels singing their dirges for him.

The Queen's birthday was celebrated by a parade of the forces, at which even the rebels were constrained to take part, for alarmed at the assembly of so many troops they opened a terrific fusillade, as much as to say "we see you and are quite ready for you." A Royal Standard was hoisted, and as soon as the troops had been drawn up in line facing the fort, the Governor, dressed in his civil uniform, left the fort and was received with a salute. After an inspection, the Governor, placing himself in front of the line, gave the command to advance in review order; then, having halted, a royal salute was given, and finally three ringing cheers for the Queen. It was an impressive sight to witness this act of homage to our Queen in the heart of a hostile country, with crowds of savage natives hemming us in on every side, but the love of all towards her is strong, and wherever the flag waves the loyal respect due to her is not forgotten. The cheers raised before the fort at Kumassi by the white officers and the native troops serving with them were certainly as heartfelt as any that were given elsewhere on that day. At the close of the parade all the officers came on to the veranda, and there we drank the Queen's health, feeling assured of her sympathy with us in our extremity.

Several foraging parties were from time to time sent out in search of food, and to let the rebels know we were not asleep. All the stockades around Kumassi, with the sole exception of that on the Patassi road, which later we were to break through, were visited, and although information was gained, we were never successful in getting food. The lack of a plentiful supply of ammunition prevented any hard fighting, and as soon as the rebels appeared in force the troops had to be recalled. On one occasion it was determined to attack the stockade on the Mampon road just before the first glimmer of light appeared in the skies. The idea was that the rebels manning the stockade would be surprised, and that our troops, after rushing it, should wheel round to the left, and supported by a further force, take the camp in the rear before the rebels could recover, and so enable our people to seize all the food within reach. Volunteers were called for, and specially instructed in the work which lay before them. The officer in command was very pleased with the result, and on the eventful morning led them forth, as he hoped, to glory and victory. They started at 4.30 a.m., looking like spectres as they glided through the mist. Hope ran high, and we who were listening at the fort for the signal for reinforcements to follow, could not understand why it was not given. The mystery was explained, for again through the mist appeared the same phantom forms, the officer with bowed head. His men had failed him, and at the critical moment had lost nerve. There was some excuse for this, for as they neared the stockade they found themselves making continual crackling noises with their feet, the ground all around having been strewn with dried wood and cocoanut shell, placed there purposely by the rebels to give an alarm, and a little further on they encountered thin ropes hung with bells, which when touched jingled weirdly. Their superstitious minds, already over-strained by lack of food, made them imagine all kinds of uncanny things. They halted, and the chance of taking the stockade was gone. The rebels were on the alert, and the officer was re-luctantly compelled to bring them back.

A very sad day for us was the 29th May, when Captain Maguire was shot through the heart while with one of the armed foraging parties. He was a gallant and popular officer, deservedly liked by all. He was laid to rest by the side of Captain Middle-mist, all his comrades following him with sorrow in their hearts. It was a military funeral, and the Roman Catholic prayers for the dead were read by the Governor over the grave. Many were the tributes of esteem and love laid upon his coffin, all made from the beautiful roses which have been induced to grow in dreary Kumassi. The native kings and chiefs attended the funeral, and thus testified their regard for an officer whom they knew to be brave and true.

Brave Hearts and True

The weary, weary days wore on. No nearer seemed the relief which we were sure must have been sent to us. No news beyond native rumours, now getting fewer and fewer, for the people were too weak and languid to go far for it, and the risk was also greater, as the rebels grew daily more confident and aggressive. Things looked very black and dismal. The rains were in full force. Europeans and natives were constantly ill from the unwholesome and unnutritious food; familiar faces were daily showing signs of privation and starvation; the doctors had their hands full; and to add to our distress small-pox broke out among the natives. The drugs and medical comforts were served out with the strictest economy, and only the most pressing cases among the natives and refugees could be relieved.

One day, coming in from our evening stroll, I saw a little boy lying by the side of the road, starvation written on his face. I called one of my servants, and told him to bring what had been left from our so-called luncheon. It was a handful of mince made from the ration beef, and a small piece of biscuit. I gave it to the child, waiting to see if he would eat it. He clutched at it ravenously, and put it to his mouth, but was too far gone to eat it. He died that night. This was only one of many such cases too pitiful to record. Knowing what it was myself to feel hungry, trembling all over from weakness and want of food, my heart went out to these poor starving people around me, and what could be spared I gave, but what was it? Infinitesimal! The state of the refugees had become very pitiful. Leaves from the trees, grass, anything that was thought eatable was eagerly sought for, and converted into food; all around us people were dying. I often had the pain of seeing a man sitting in the road suddenly fall forward dead. Most terrible of all was to see those who from starvation had gone mad. The shrieks and yells of some of them were heartrending; others would quietly sit down, perhaps picking and tearing their cloths to pieces, with a vacant smile upon their faces in which each bone could almost be defined.

A soup kitchen was started to feed some hundred and fifty children every morning. The soup—indeed it was only an apology for soup —was made from the crumbs of biscuits left in the tins and any scraps that could be spared from the various tables. Long before the time to serve out this daily ration the poor wee things would take their places by the roadside and clamour for it, holding out their tins with great impatience. As much as ten shillings was offered for a rat, but rats, lizards, parrots, dogs and pets of all kinds had long since disappeared. It was now when the stress of hunger was most pressing that many of the women and the children went over to the rebels, preferring slavery with food to liberty with starvation. Who could blame them? It certainly looked as if those who had thrown in their lot with the rebels would be the gainers, for the all-powerful white man seemed powerless now, and faith in him was waning. I often wondered whether the loyal kings and chiefs regretted standing by the Government. I think they must have done so more than once in their innermost hearts, for they suffered considerably, as did their followers.

The kings often came to see me, and the visits were really quite amusing. The King of Aguna was my most frequent guest, and would walk round and round the room making absurd remarks about things that took his fancy. He was a very thirsty soul, and found it an immense privation not being able to get his usual supply of refreshment. He was always given a drink on his visits to me, but the heaviness of his hand in helping himself

was alarming, and we had to point out to our kingly guest that he must not be quite so liberal to himself now that comforts were so scarce and precious. One day his two wives, driven by hunger, thought the rebel camp more comfortable, and deserted him. The King was greatly annoyed, and found himself much laughed at by the more fortunate, but he became philosophic at last and once more regained his spirits. We tried as best we could to prevent our spirits falling to zero by having what we called "starvation" dinner-parties, followed by a game of cards, and one afternoon I was entertained at tea by two of the officers whose duty it was to be on guard at the Bantama stockade. It was quite an event in the monotonous routine of my daily life, and how I laughed over the bread and jam sandwiches! The bread, which was to be the attractive delicacy, was, alas! only bread by courtesy, and was but another disappointment added to our many others.

CHAPTER XII

A FORLORN HOPE

AT last the time came when we seemed to give up all hope of being relieved. Our scanty stock of rations was nearing the end, and we had to begin to make preparations for departure. We talked now of "the march out," and not of when the relieving column would reach us, as we had before. Our spies, thinking perhaps to please us, would report that the white man's troops were close to us, and would be in "to-morrow, or the next day." At first we were inclined to believe these accounts, and prayed that they might be true; but as each day ended and nothing came of them, we began to realise that our only hope of life lay in the hazardous experiment of trying to force our way through the rebel lines.

One of the reports brought in only a few days before we had to take the momentous march was to the effect that the advance guard of the relief column was at Ordahsu, that five posts had been

A Forlorn Hope

established between Esumeja and that place, that the officer commanding at Ordahsu was waiting for the main body to come up ; that he had sent a letter by a Krooboy to the Governor, and that the boy had got as far as Karsi, where he was captured and the letter taken from him. He further reported that the letter was read by a scholar in the rebel camp, and was to the effect that the advance guard was at Ordahsu, that the order was not to advance until the "main body" arrived, and that the Governor was to be patient. In the light of later intelligence as to the movements of the "main body," the report was probably a correct one.

A few cases of stores and wines belonging to officers in the Northern Territories, which when the Ashantis rose were waiting at Kumassi for transmission to them, had been commandeered by order of the Governor, no one being allowed to buy more than his share. These stores had now come to an end, and had it not been for this slender addition to our ration fare we must have indeed suffered more terribly than we did.

Three or four days before we left we gave the rebels a few parting shots, and listened I am sorry to say with pleasure to a most unearthly yell that came from the camp into which we had fired the

A Forlorn Hope

first of the rockets. We came to the conclusion that *hundreds* of Ashantis must have succumbed to that rocket, whereas, I expect, if we had seen the result, the only damage was a scare and stampede.

The date of departure was kept very secret, no one knowing either that or the road we were to take. Even now, although we had steeled our hearts for the final act, it was impossible not to allow our thoughts to stray back to the old topic of relief. Many a time during our evening walks did I scan the road leading to Cape Coast for any sign of approaching succour. Once as I gazed I saw in the distance an impudent rebel sentry come out of the bush on to the road and flaunt his impertinent independence by executing a war dance. It was his first and last *pas-de-seul.*

Although unknown, the date fixed for our departure was the 23rd June. On the 22nd news, which after having being carefully sifted seemed to be authentic, was brought in, to the effect that the relief column was so near to us that it must arrive within two days. The Governor and Major Morris thereupon consulted together whether to believe it or to treat it as a not wholly reliable native rumour. The latter course was decided upon, and this was well, for there was only a three days' supply of rations for everyone left, and the relieving column, as the sequel proved, had still to consume twenty-three days before it reached Kumassi. The order as to the march out of the bulk of the troops, and as to the garrison to be left behind to guard the fort and the flag were not, under the circumstances, counter-manded, but Captain Bishop, who was to be left in command of the garrison, was told of the news by the Governor, and of the feeling which both he and Major Morris had that it was reliable to the extent that a relief column was drawing towards Kumassi and might confidently be expected to arrive some days before the 15th July, the date up to which provisions for the little garrison were to be left. So it was that our death-in-life existence came to an end on the 23rd June. We felt that our lives were to be offered for the task of up-holding the British flag, and it was with sinking hearts that we wished good-bye and good luck to our comrades who were to be left in the fort. The Governor's last words, which expressed the general feeling, were, "well, you have a supply of food for twenty-three days and are safe for that period, but we are going to die to-day." The account given to

A Forlorn Hope

Reuter's representative by Captain Bishop of what happened after we left is as follows :—

"When the column marched out of Kumassi on the morning of Saturday, June 23rd, we were assured that authentic information had been received that the relief force was at Esumeja, and that we should be relieved in five days at the very latest. Left alone, our first task was to take stock of our food-supply, and then to tell off the men to their various positions in the bastions and so forth, warning them that they were on no account to leave the guns, but always to sleep beside them. Every man had one hundred and twenty Martini-Metford cartridges, with a reserve of fifty per man. Major Morris had scarcely left Kumassi when we saw a band of Ashantis coming towards the fort from the Bantama stockade. I suppose they thought that the fort was evacuated, but the fire from two Maxims soon convinced them that such was not the case, and after firing a random volley they retired.

"It will be remembered that the friendly population, coast people, traders, and so forth had fixed up shelters all round the fort under fire of our guns. These, to the number of some thousands, extended for a considerable distance, and were now abandoned, all of the people, with the exception of about one hundred and fifty, having gone away with the Governor's column. These empty shelters

formed a pestilential area, the stench from which
was such that, despite the heat, we were compelled
to keep the windows of the fort shut. Moreover,
they now formed a fine cover for the Ashantis,
and we had to set to work to destroy them. The
grass structures had been so sodden by the tropical
rains that it was not until June 27th we were able
to burn out this plague spot.

"Apart from the stench, the presence of hundreds of vultures afforded only too sure evidence
of what some of these huts contained, but to make
certain that there were no half-dead people a
personal inspection of the shelters was necessary.
So Ralph and I, each with a handkerchief tied over
our faces, and half a dozen men visited the huts.
We found decaying remains on all sides, and many
bodies which had been torn to pieces by the
vultures. In one hut we found a wretched starving
woman who had been living for three days with
her dead child beside her.

"In the meantime starvation was doing its work
in the fort. The day after the Governor's column
left three of our men died, and almost daily one
or more succumbed. The gates of the fort were
never opened except for a few minutes at early
morning, and again at dusk, when the dead were
carried out and buried in the adjoining trench, no
one being strong enough to dig graves. For the
first five days we were not unduly anxious, but
when no relief came as promised, and we remem-

bered that we had been told that a force was only sixteen miles off, our spirits fell, and after ten days we gave up all hope. Neither of us thought we should survive, but we kept up an appearance of cheerfulness for the sake of our men, who bore their sufferings with the greatest fortitude. I regard the conduct of the native troops as marvellous; they maintained perfect discipline and never complained. Our first business every morning was to serve out the rations to the men, who came up to the table one by one. Some were too weak to do this and lay about on the ground.

"All were worn to skin and bone, but there were a few who, to relieve their hunger, had been eating poisonous herbs, which caused great swellings over the body. At last the rations consisted of a cup of linseed meal and a block of tinned meat about two inches square. Occasionally some native women would come outside the fort and offer, at ridiculous prices, certain articles of food. These were greedily purchased, and many would have readily given three times the price asked. A piece of coco, usually costing the fraction of a penny, realised fifteen shillings, and bananas fetched eighteen-pence each. I paid fifteen shillings for a tiny pine-apple. But even these high-priced luxuries were extremely rare, and the value of money can be judged when I tell you I used to pay the Hausa troops three shillings in lieu of half a biscuit. By this means we saved a few biscuits, and the Hausas were able to purchase leaves, etc., for food. A large quantity of our scanty store of biscuits had been so badly packed that they were full of weevils and grubs, while others were thickly coated with mildew.

"Every two or three days our anxieties were increased by reports that the loyal Bekwais and N'Kwantas had joined the Ashantis, and were encamped two days' outside the town. We were also told that the Governor's column had been cut up, and that the Ashantis had a white man's head in their camp. Now, to make matters worse, small-pox broke out in the fort, and we had to remove the cases to a hut under the fort wall. Every day Dr. Hay, although extremely ill, clambered over the wall to visit these cases, and, in doing so, again contracted fever. As a last resource I tried to get some messages through to Bekwai. Going to the treasury, I took out a bag containing a hundred pounds, and offered it to the first man who would deliver a message at Esumeja, sixteen miles off. Two Lagos men volunteered, but returned without success. Several times the Ashantis came out from their stockades—once to burn the Basel Mission Chapel, which we tried ineffectually to save ; and once to destroy the Wesleyan Church, which, being in a hollow, was out of our line of fire. At night small bands prowled about near the fort, and round the small-pox hospital, which we had to remove.

"On July 14th the usual native stories were told

A Forlorn Hope

of distant firing, but these reports, which, by their constant repetition, had at first caused us to hope, only made us more despondent. On the evening of that day the native officer said he was sure he had heard a 7-pounder, and we fired three double shells as a signal, but there was no reply, and we felt sure that the supposed 7-pounder was only an Ashanti Dane gun. Next morning when I was in the bastion I distinctly heard three volleys fired in the direction of the Cape Coast road. Even then we were not quite sure of their origin, but we felt more hopeful. The men were quite apathetic, being too weak to care much for anything. At 4.30 in the afternoon we heard terrific firing, which removed any doubts we had, and after opening a pint bottle of champagne—one of our few remaining medical comforts—we mounted the look-out, field glasses in hand. It was very pathetic that even with relief at hand some of the men were just at the point of death. At 4.45, amid the din of the ever-approaching firing, we heard ringing British cheers, and a shell passed over the top of the fort, which was in the direct line of fire. We then saw shells bursting in all directions about 400 yards off, and we fired a Maxim to show that we were alive. Then to our intense relief we heard a distant bugle sound the 'Halt!' and at six o'clock on Sunday evening, July 15th, we saw the heads of the advance guard emerge from the bush with a fox terrier trotting gaily in front. Instantly the two

GIRLS GRINDING CORN

Face page 192

A Forlorn Hope

buglers on the veranda sounded the 'Welcome,' blowing it over and over again in their excitement. A few minutes later a group of white helmets told us of the arrival of the staff, and we rushed out of the fort cheering to the best of our ability. The meeting with our rescuers was of a most affecting character. Colonel Willcocks and his officers plainly showed what they had gone through. The whole of the force was halted in front of the fort, and three cheers for the Queen and the waving of caps and helmets formed an evening scene that none of us will ever forget."

So ended one of the five historic sieges of 1900. The siege of Kumassi, it must be remembered, took place in one of the worst climates in the world. The enemy was a savage and bloodthirsty one, and our only defenders were black troops, many of them but recruits and inexperienced. Throughout we were short of ammunition, and our little force of 33 Europeans and some 720 Hausas opposed thousands of natives. I think it not wrong to say that all did their duty nobly and well. Weakened in body by want of food, and with the mental strain upon us which was inseparable from our position, and which in the West African climate never fails to tell upon health, there was not once any sign of failure or despair.

CHAPTER XIII

OUR ESCAPE FROM KUMASSI

AT last the dreaded hour came when our shelter for eight and a half weeks had to be left. Dark indeed were our prospects when it became necessary to quit this refuge, and to face fresh danger in the open. Starvation, a bitter enemy against which we had fought day by day, was driving us forth to meet another and as merciless a foe. So'worn were we, and so weary in mind and body, that anything seemed better at last than the dreariness of those days that brought us no news of approaching relief and rescue. The sleepless nights of mental agony gone through, the preparations for departure overshadowed by thoughts of torture and death, were now things of the past, and when the summons came that Kumassi was to be left within three hours a great load seemed lifted, and we, trusting to an all-merciful Providence, went forth to meet our fate. The motto "God helps those who help themselves"

Our Escape from Kumassi

was fully justified in our case. We *were* helping ourselves, and how great was His help to us!

Many plans and contrivances had been suggested for protecting our hammocks against the enemy's fire, but none proved of any service. A number of sheets of corrugated iron were stored in the fort for roofing and other purposes, and it was thought they might be used as a kind of armour to the hammocks, provided the additional weight was not too much for the bearers, and also if they would withstand the rebel slugs. The idea was to bend these sheets into the shape of a V, so that when passed over the hammock-pole they would fall on either side of the hammock, like the roof of a house; but experiments proved them to be useless, and in any case it is more than doubtful if the hammock-men would have been able to carry the additional weight. It gave us an afternoon's amusement trying them. Several sheets were placed at various distances and fired at by the friendly native levies, whom I have before mentioned. The slugs went through the sheets as if they were paper, and in the end the hammocks were left as they always are, no special protection being found practicable.

Major Morris and the Governor had many con-

sultations together about the arrangements, but no
one knew what was being discussed. If I ventured
to ask, my answer always was, "oh, we have been
having a chat together." At last the Governor
confided to me that all was settled, and that we
were really to start on Saturday, June 23rd. I had
all along thought that we should have to make an
attempt to break through the rebel lines, and had
tried to school myself to it, but I must confess that
when the announcement was made my heart sank
within me, for I knew what the risks were, and
what horrors awaited us if the attempt should fail.
I tried nevertheless to appear cheerful, and I hope
that it was not without success, for I felt that now,
if at any time, dejection must be thrust aside, so
that all of our little band of Europeans might rally
for the final and supreme venture.

I remember asking whether the fort was to be
abandoned, and if the flag, which we had so jeal-
ously guarded during the long and weary weeks,
was to be hauled down and Kumassi given up
to the rebels. It was a relief to learn that this
was not to be, and that a force sufficient to main-
tain itself in the fort against attack would be left
under two European officers and one native officer,
with provisions sufficient for twenty-four days. The

Our Escape from Kumassi

sick and wounded men of the Hausa force were also to be left under the charge of one of the doctors. All the reports brought to us by our spies pointed to the near approach of a relieving column, and both my husband and Major Morris thought that these reports could be relied upon, and that it should not take a column more than twenty-four days to defeat the rebels and reach its destination. Their calculations proved very exact, for the garrison within the fort successfully held out against attack, and was relieved on the twenty-third day.

The night of the 22nd of June will ever remain graven upon my memory. It was necessary to get as much rest as possible before the momentous day which was to decide our fate, and we all went to bed as usual, after we had finished getting our loads ready for the carriers. At 2.30 a.m. the word was quietly sent round to all that the march would commence at 5 a.m., and that everyone must be in his assigned place in the column of route by that hour. Most of the carriers had slept in or near the fort yard for several nights so that they might be on the spot, and also to throw dust into the people's eyes as to the actual date of departure. These carriers on being awakened made a fiendish noise, which all entreaties could not stop. Collecting loads did not take very long, and at about 4.30 the carriers were sitting in the road, each with the load allotted to him. The loyal kings and chiefs and their followers were in a greatly excited state, running hither and thither collecting such goods and chattels as they were allowed to take with them, for no semblance of state, such as a king's umbrella or palanquin, was to be admitted to the column. Then there were the poor refugees, who, if they had strength enough to march, were allowed to follow behind the rearguard. Well, the noise of all those thousands can perhaps be imagined, but cannot be described. Our great anxiety was that this awful hubbub might let the camps around Kumassi know that something unusual was taking place, and so put them on the alert. As if by magic the noise suddenly ceased, and the arrival of the troops was silently awaited.

The detachments from their various barracks were to fall into their places at the fort gates. No one except the officers, Major Morris, and the Governor knew which road we were to take. Everyone who had not been privately advised thought that it was to be the Cape Coast road, and even in this dark hour an incident occurred to raise a laugh. The plan of the march had been typed and handed round, everyone being told to get into place quietly and quickly. Mr. Ramseyer, the Basel missionary, presuming we were going down the Cape Coast road, had collected and placed his party just upon the spot from which the advance guard was to move off. The Governor seeing this called up his private secretary and said, "tell Mr. Ramseyer he must keep his place in the column, and not get in the way of the advance guard." I was standing by at the time, and I whispered, "but he is all right; he doesn't know we are going the opposite way!" So we three had a little laugh together, as the show at the last moment was nearly given away—and by the Governor himself! Mr. Ramseyer was, however, judiciously made to fall in nearer to where he would have to start from.

It was a cold, damp, depressing morning, and Kumassi was enveloped in a blue-white mist, which hung like a death shadow over all. We had, of course, to dress by lamplight, and to have what little breakfast was possible by the same light. I can in imagination now see myself sitting at the table cutting a Bologna sausage. It was the last one of our stores, and had been saved up for this dreaded but expected moment. The sausage was in a tin which had in the hurry been badly opened, and it would not allow itself to be pushed out; the poor thing had a great wound in its side from the tin-opener, and every time I attempted to cut off a slice the sausage would recede. I managed, however, to cut up about half of it, and to make sandwiches with our two biscuits—our day's supply of food! The other half was put into a handy box for our next meal, if we were ever to have another, but, alas! the box was one of many thrown into the bush, and never gladdened our eyes again.

Five o'clock drew nearer and nearer. The Hausas were seen coming to form up. We went down the fort steps for the last time, with a silent prayer that all would be well with us. The advance guard moved off, under the command of Captains Armitage and Leggett; the column fell into line, and for weal or woe the march began. A deathlike silence reigned. I was told to get into my hammock; I did it like one in a dream, yet that scene, terrible in its weird solemnity, will never fade from my mind. Dr. Chalmers' allotted place in the column was by my hammock, and

Our Escape from Kumassi

from that moment until we reached Accra he never relaxed his watchful and tender care over me. I can never repay him for all his kindness, and for the cheerful encouragement he never failed to give when things looked darkest and most desperate.

We moved on down a small hill leading past the water supply until we reached one of the swamps surrounding Kumassi. It was a perfect quagmire, and progression became very slow with constant stoppages. The path became worse and worse, until it was so narrow that movement in single file became necessary ; thick dense bush lined on either side the track, which was slippery and dangerous. The tension was very great. Just as we emerged from the swamp, which, fortunately for us, was not at its worst, a poor carrier, with an ammunition box on his head, fell backwards from exhaustion, gave one gasp, and went to his long home. This was the beginning of many terrible things to happen that day. I shall never forget the sight of this unfortunate man lying on his back in a bed of rushes, his hands still clutching his load which lay uptilted against his head.

About half an hour after leaving the fort the

first shot was fired by the advance guard, showing that the rebels at the Patassi stockade were blocking our onward march and that we had met resistance. What was to be the extent of that opposition? Was it to be insuperable, were the rebels to swarm down upon us, and was I to be the witness of a hand-to-hand conflict between them and those around me? The column had halted, and except for the sound of firing in front a deathlike silence prevailed. The only movement was the restless shifting of the hammock-men; all were alert, for all knew that the supreme moment which was to decide our fate was near at hand. To be under fire in a strongly built fort is an awful experience, but can any woman who has not been through it realise what it means to be in a hammock, the trees of the forest touching you on both sides of the narrow path, and with bush so dense that thousands could be hidden in it pointing their guns at you, while you would be quite unconscious of their close proximity until the report of the guns was heard?

The enemy opened fire from their stockade as our advance guard came in sight. Then the firing went on without ceasing. Only those actually taking part in the struggle knew what was happening, and

Our Escape from Kumassi

the suspense was 'errible. We felt that the longer
the stockade was .ntaken the greater was our peril.
The rebels were beating their tom-toms and drums,
signalling upon them in native fashion for reinforcements from the neighbouring camps. They had
made a perfect circular road round Kumassi, with
camps at short intervals, so that from any point
they could communicate from camp to camp. Why
they did not do so on this occasion it is impossible
to say ; had they done so they could, humanly
speaking, have annihilated us all in a few minutes.
Thousands against our poor weakened force of six
hundred!

The firing went on for about twenty minutes,
when a triumphant shout went up from our men of
"Allah! il Allah!" Our hearts gave a jump of
joy, but only a momentary one ; for this welcome
shout was answered by the victorious war-cry of
the Ashantis, a hideous noise with which during
the siege our ears had become familiar. We did
not know what to think! At these supreme
moments of life thoughts seem dulled ; a stirring
leaf, or a pretty flower, or a man's curious pose, pin
your attention, and distract it from what is taking
place around you. I gave one cry of "we are
lost!" My dear friend, Dr. Chalmers, pushed his

way to the hammock's side, and, taking my hand, he said, "be quite calm; wait!" At this moment again our men shouted "Allah! il Allah!" and this time there was no response from the rebels. The bugle sounded the "Cease fire!" and in a few minutes the advance followed, and we moved on again. The stockade had been taken. It was a wonderful structure some six or seven feet high and three or four feet in thickness, built of gigantic forest trees laid lengthways, the interstices filled up with swish and twigs and brambles, and bound together with telegraph wire. In some of the stockades the Government iron telegraph poles had been used. The Patassi stockade had wings to it, which extended into the bush on either side, and were thus hidden from sight, but the front had been cleared so as to give the occupants of it a clear view forward. Like other stockades round Kumassi it had been carefully loopholed, and in every way prepared for defence with considerable skill and ingenuity.

Our guns were not powerful enough to take it by a frontal attack, the 7-pounders, as before mentioned, being absolutely useless against these stockades; besides, the time which it takes to get the guns into action could ill be spared in our hurried flight.

Our Escape from Kumassi

A brisk fire was kept up, under cover of which an enfilading movement was made to the right through the bush. Fortunately the undergrowth here was not as dense as usual, and the men were able to push through it. Resistance in force was expected, and Captain Leggett, who was in command, was astonished to find that he was getting through without it. The reason was soon apparent. The rebels were imitating our tactics. They too had determined to try a flank attack, and poured out of the stockade on our left, little expecting that we were working round on the other side and getting close up to it. A charge led by Captain Leggett brought our men right into the stockade before the rebels realised what had happened. Then it was that the Hausas raised their shouts of "Allah! il Allah!" to be answered by the war cries of the rebels. So scared were the rebels at seeing the Hausas suddenly in their midst that, abandoning their flank attack, they turned and fled, several falling to the rifle fire of our men. So the stockade was taken. It was a smart piece of work and quickly done. This success, which to us was of the utmost value, inasmuch as it enabled us to push through the cordon drawn by the rebels around Kumassi, had the effect of raising the spirits of our men, and materially assisted us in overcoming the resistance which we were yet to meet.

The order was that upon the stockade being taken an opening through it was to be made, to allow the column to pass on quickly. This was by no means an easy task, because of the really excellent way in which it had been constructed, and it was only found possible to remove the top of it in one place. However by placing logs on the ground close to this partial opening it was easy to climb up and get over. I found it somewhat like negotiating a rather difficult English stile. I should like to have carefully examined the stockade, which appeared to me to show considerable ingenuity and hard work, giving evidence that the Ashantis are not only clever, but when put to it energetic; but there was no time, there was only opportunity for a hurried and cursory glance, as we had to push on. I have heard military men who have seen them express their opinion that the construction of the Ashanti stockades would be hard to beat. It is said that the Ashantis were much struck by the laagers made by the troops during the Ashanti expedition of 1896, and made mental notes of them, and that their education in stockades was perfected by the Mendis from Sierra Leone, who were brought into the Colony early in 1897 to act as carriers to officers making their way to the country beyond and to the north of Ashanti, now known as the Northern Territories. This is by no means unlikely, as stockades were a feature of the rebellion in Sierra Leone in 1898, and the Mendi carriers, finding the work which they had contracted for irksome, deserted, and for a long time roamed through Ashanti picking up a precarious livelihood as best they could.

Corps Furnishing Troops.	ORDER OF MARCH.	Number of Carriers.
Accra and Kumassi Hausas.	. . . 2 men and a Lance Corporal.	
	100 yds.	
	10 men and a good N.C.O.	
	100 yds.	
	100 men in the ranks with Native Officer and Company Sergeant Major under Captains Armitage and Leggett	16 (2 H)
Gun detachments to be furnished by Gambaga Hausas.	1 7-Pounder	12
	1 Maxim	8
	2 loads of Double shell	2
	1 load of Shrapnel „	1
	2 loads of Case Shot	2
	1 load of Powder Charges with sufficient Friction Tubes	1
	2 Boxes of ·303 Maxim Ammunition	2
Gambaga Hausas.	50 Gambaga Hausas rank and file under Mr. Berthon	8
	1 Medical Officer (Dr. Graham), 3 native hammocks, 1 dispenser, and 1 carrier with dressings	21 (H)
	50 Gambaga Hausas, under Mr. Iddi Bakanu.	
	Major Morris, & Doctor Garland	
	Capt. Marshall and 1 Dresser	25 (3 H)
	1 carrier with dressings	
	25 Gambaga Hausas, under Captain Digan	8 (H)
	His Excellency, and Lady Hodgson	16 (2 H)
	Doctor Chalmers	8 (H)
	20 Gold Coast Constabulary.	

Fifty Northern Territories Hausas and Thirty Gold Coast Hausas.	* These Hausas will be distributed amongst the carriers in parties of ten under a non-commissioned officer.	
	* Hausas under Captain Parmeter.	
	220 Carriers.	
	Reserve Ammunition. N.T. Hausas	21
	Northern Territories Baggage	72
	Dr. Tweedie with reserve hammocks and Medical requirements	39
	Gold Coast Baggage	25
	Mr. Branch, 18 (3 loads of picks, shovels, & felling axes)	18
	Spare	45
		220
		220
		350

Our Escape from Kumassi

Corps Furnishing Troops.	ORDER OF MARCH—*continued.*	Number of Carriers.
Gold Coast Hausas.	20 Gold Coast Hausas.	350
	Maxim Gun, furnished by Lagos Hausas . .	8
	10 Boxes ·450 Maxim Ammunition . . .	10
Lagos Hausas.	* These Hausas will be distributed amongst the carriers in parties of ten under a non-commissioned officer.	8 (H)
	* 70 Lagos Hausas about under Captain Reid.	
	Missionaries . . . **52**	
	Lagos Hausas' Baggage . **31**	260
	His Excellency's Baggage, with Private Secretary's . **106**	
	Dr. Chalmer's Baggage . **21**	
	Carriers belonging to Mr. David and Mr. Grundy.	
	Spare Carriers . **50**	
	All the Clerks and persons belonging to the above baggage, including the Civil Police.	
	Native Kings.	
	25 Hausas under Captain Cochrane . . .	8 (H)
	Rear Guard.	
	1 Medical Officer (Dr. Macfarlane) . . .	8 (H)
	3 Native hammocks . . .	12
	1 Dispenser.	
	1 Carrier, with dressings . . .	1
	3 loads of Double shell . . .	3
	1 load of Shrapnel shell . . .	1
	5 loads of Case Shot . . .	5
	1 load of Powder Charges . . .	1
	10 Boxes of ·450 Maxim Ammunition . .	10
	1 7-Pounder . . .	12
	1 ·450 Maxim . . .	8
	50 Lagos Hausas under Captain Aplin, C.M.G. .	8 (H)
		713

L. MORRIS, MAJOR,

Commanding Troops.

KUMASSI, *June 17th*, 1900.

CHAPTER XIV

THROUGH FIRE AND FLOOD

AFTER passing through the stockade we came upon a perfect little camp. A large space had been cleared of bush, and beneath the shade of the forest trees had been erected small beehive-looking huts, each sufficiently large to accommodate at least four men. Before every hut a fire was burning and food cooking, showing that at the time of our arrival the enemy were engaged in preparations for a meal, and having neglected to send out scouts to watch our proceedings at Kumassi were wholly unprepared for our appearance. The temptation to our hammock-men and carriers, who had not had a square meal for weeks, to fall upon the good things they saw was more than they could withstand. The close proximity of the rebels, and the danger attending a separation from the force, passed unheeded in the imperative craving to satisfy hunger. It was to them the pressing necessity of the moment, and persuasion, threats, and the employment of even sterner measures to endeavour to prevent loss of life proved in many cases useless. Poor fellows! It was piteous to see their hunger, but more piteous still to see them satisfying it at the risk of their lives. Many of them we never again saw, for, lingering behind the column, they fell easy victims to the enemy.

There were many signs that the Ashantis had received that morning a very fair punishment, for several dead bodies were lying about along the road, although many of them had been cleared out of the way by the advance guard, so as not to impede the progress of the column when it began to move after the capture of the stockade. The column was about two miles long, so that at the time of the action at the stockade the rearguard had not left the fort gates. Why the Ashantis did not swarm from their various camps into Kumassi then and there, and massacre the fugitives following the rearguard, will ever remain a testimony to the slowness of the working of the native mind, and also to the direct interposition of Providence. Nothing was easier for them to do, and we feared it would be done.

Soon after passing through the camp at the

back of the stockade the village of Patassi was reached, and there more fighting took place. The rebels were, however, soon cleared out, and on and on we went, hearing shots fired either by the advance guard or by the rearguard. In one of the villages passed through, all of which had to be cleared of the rebels, who in many cases vacated only to make a determined stand in the bush a few hundred yards further on, I fell out of my hammock. How I did this stupid thing it is impossible to say, except that the hammock had become tilted from crushing through the bushes. At this moment the firing in front was very heavy, and there was no time to be lost. It takes some time as a rule to settle oneself comfortably in a hammock, but that was not to be thought of now. In I had to bundle as best I could, and the hammock-men had to run to come in touch again with those in front. I took care not to do this sort of thing again. Skirts are an impediment when fleeing for your life in Ashanti-land, and for once I felt myself in agreement with Lady Harberton's views on rational dress.

After marching for about four hours the "Halt!" was sounded, so as to give a little rest to all, and to find out how the rear of the column had fared.

A STREET IN AKROPONG

Face page 216

Through Fire and Flood

We halted in a small plantation village, Hausas being posted at all points to keep a good look-out. Bananas and plantains were growing profusely, but not much time was allowed to gather them. Hearty congratulations were passed round on our good luck in advancing thus far alive, and inquiries were made as to the various experiences encountered on the way. It was here that I heard that Captain Leggett had been badly wounded at the stockade, and had since been carried. Poor fellow! He looked fairly comfortable in his hammock, yet how one longed to be able really to help his sufferings with comforts and care which it was impossible to give or even obtain! I was terribly distressed, for already another of our brave officers, Captain Marshall of the Royal West Kent Regiment, had received his death-blow. He ran past my hammock early in the morning on his way to the front, cheering me by saying that everything was going on splendidly; his face was keen with excitement, and he even had time as he passed to give his usual merry laugh. Ten minutes after that I saw one of the doctors kneeling down by the side of an officer dressing his wound, and to my dismay I learnt in answer to my question, "who is it?" that it was Captain Marshall. It seemed too terrible that only ten minutes before he had been speaking to me in health and strength, and now he was lying helpless, and as it afterwards proved mortally wounded. He had been hit in the head by a stray shot from the bush just after passing my hammock.

The march was resumed after about twenty minutes' halt, such time for refreshment having been taken by those who had been thoughtful enough to put something in their pockets. My Bologna sausage was once more in requisition, but although we were desperately hungry, only half of the sandwiches were used, and the remainder were reserved for a subsequent meal. We went on again with a more hopeful spirit, having done well so far, and halting once more about two o'clock rested an hour. Here it was that the remainder of my sandwiches went, for there were many who were only too glad to share them with me. The village in which we made this halt did not inspire me with confidence, for the bush came right up to it, and from the fact that the advance guard had had rather a struggle to get in we felt that the enemy were watching all our doings, and had the advantage of seeing us without being seen. Here the whole column closed up, and we heard that the rearguard had had a warm time of it; but a warmer one still was in store, for as we left this village the rebels made a desperate attack. The rearguard fought well, but was not able to save a panic amongst the carriers, who threw away their loads in order to be better able, as they thought, to save themselves. Many of them were killed, and our goods and chattels were lost to us for ever.

We reached our destination for the night about 6 p.m. The advance guard, which all the day long had had a very busy time, were not destined to get in without a struggle. Terrebum, where the night was spent, was found to be occupied by the rebels in strong force. All the huts facing the approach to the village had been loopholed, and it appeared as if we were to have a struggle for possession as severe as that over the Patassi stockade. The noise of firing was incessant and seemed close by us, for at this time the column had closed up, and the main body behind which we were marching was supporting the firing line.

Darkness was coming on when a victorious shout announced that the rebels had been cleared out. Rain had now begun to fall, and we were all tired, wet, miserable, and hungry. The village huts were intolerably filthy, but there was no help for it; in we had to go for the rain was increasing, and the village was being filled to overflowing with the people forming our column. Shall I ever forget the scene which met my eye when I stepped out of my hammock? It beggars description. There were not more than ten huts in all. These had been told off for the Europeans, so that the Hausas, the loyal kings and chiefs with their followers, the hammock-men and carriers, and the many refugees who had come on with us had to find places for themselves in the open. Already the advance guard and main body had been disposed around the village so as to be able to repel any attack. Others were pressing in. The whole ground was a quagmire, everything was wet, and it seemed to be impossible to find anywhere a dry spot to sit down upon. When at last all had come in, crowded into the narrow space were some two thousand five hundred people packed as closely as sardines in a tin. Children were crying, men squabbling for room, misery and hunger written large on every face. It was a scene which can, I fear, never fade from my memory.

Just before daylight finally failed the rebels thought it a fitting time to make an attack on us.

Through Fire and Flood

They opened a terrific fire from the bush which as usual came quite close up to the village. Fortunately their aim was too high to do any damage, and their slugs passed over our heads. I confess to having felt very nervous, wondering whether, if the attack were pressed home, the panic which must have seized the unarmed portion of our column would be our annihilation. Volleys were being fired by the Hausas under the direction of their officers, and I knew from the steadiness of their fire that they were well in hand. The Maxims were being brought to bear upon the enemy when suddenly the heavens opened and poured forth a deluge of rain. It was too much for the rebels; the priming of their guns must have become so wet as to render them useless, and the firing ceased. This deluge of rain was probably our salvation. It continued all the night through, but oh, how it added to our misery!

A few of our personal loads had come in, and in one of the boxes was a tin of soup which our cook managed somehow to heat for us. It was all we had, but I doubt if I ever felt more grateful for anything in my life. Only one of our two stretcher beds was forthcoming, the other having been among the loads abandoned on the road. The same fate had overtaken our bedding and blankets, for we never saw them after leaving Kumassi. We were in a terrible plight. After much difficulty a candle was found, by the flickering light of which we ate our soup and prepared for the night. Our hut was very small and entirely open to the rain on one side. Across this we managed to fix up a waterproof sheet which I had with me in my hammock, and so kept out the rain. The stretcher bed took up nearly all the available space, but there was just room enough left for a small chair which one of the officers very good-naturedly lent us, and in which my husband on this and many subsequent nights managed to get some rest. The ground in front of our hut was ankle deep in water; everything and everybody was wet through. Throughout the night the natives kept up a continuous chatter, and the Ashantis were beating their war drums in the distance. Nothing more dismal, desolate, and discouraging can be imagined. Sheer exhaustion gave me fitful doses, but always with dreams that the Ashantis were pursuing me, and I woke up to know that they were not without foundation, for could I not hear the incessant beating of their drums.

It was a relief when the bugle sounded the

Through Fire and Flood

"Fall in!" at dawn. This was answered by the rebels firing off their guns, and in this way letting us know that they were near by and on the alert. The rain had abated a little, but a steady downpour still continued. A very dejected crowd it was that started that morning. Only with great difficulty could the column be formed up for the march according to the prescribed order, the available space being so small and the people packed so tightly that it was impossible to prevent their pushing and crowding and impeding the movements of the troops. All was, however, ready by 6.30 a.m., and we started, having had nothing to eat beyond a mouthful of bread and a small piece of ham, accompanied by very inferior coffee, which the cook had fortunately for us put into a bundle of his clothes carried by himself. He brought it to us in a tin cup, which to me looked far from clean. There was no milk and sugar. It is in my experience a fallacy to suppose that when one is starving fastidiousness as to food, or the receptacle in which it is placed, ceases. To me it was accentuated. I shall always remember the feeling of horror with which I put this unappetising cup to my lips.

CHAPTER XV

LOSSES IN THE BUSH

THE second day of our march was a very arduous one, but the advance guard was not attacked to any great extent; it had, in fact, only to encounter a few stray shots. The rebels had turned their attention to the rearguard and to the carriers, hoping for plunder, which, alas! they were successful in obtaining, for on this day nearly all the remaining boxes were lost. We arrived after ten hours' march at the stopping-place for the night, wet through, and having had nothing to eat all day, and anxiously awaited the carriers, not then knowing what had happened. It began to be whispered that very few loads were likely to come in, that the rearguard had been severely engaged, and that the carriers, again panic-stricken, had thrown away their loads in their headlong flight. I may mention that the rule with regard to carriers in bush-fighting is that when the firing commences they all put their loads on the ground and lie flat down, but unfortunately our carriers proved the exception to the rule, and we were terrible sufferers in consequence.

It appears that after leaving Terrebum the rebels came on in force, so that the rearguard had to stand a very fierce attack. The refugees following the column, panic-stricken and anxious for safety, rushed along the road overturning everything in their way. The formation of the Hausas composing the rearguard was for a time upset, but quickly recovering themselves they formed up to resist the attack. It was during this rush of the refugees that the carriers, thinking that the rearguard had been overcome by the enemy, lost their heads, and throwing down their loads, joined the general stampede, only stopping when they came upon the main body. This attack on the rearguard lasted for some time—until, in fact, the rebels came upon the loads abandoned by the carriers, when, probably thinking that more was to be gained from loot than from fighting, they dropped off to examine the loads, and the firing ceased.

We heard afterwards at Accra from one of our carriers who had been a prisoner in the rebel camp, but had succeeded in making his escape, that this attack was conducted by the Ashanti chief Antoa

Losses in the Bush

Mensa, who had 1,500 Ashantis with him. He had been detailed by the Ashanti rebel leaders, as soon as they became aware that the bulk of the Kumassi garrison had broken through their lines at Patassi, to follow the column, and if possible to stop its progress out of Ashanti, but in any case to bring back the Governor's head. They found the task too difficult, and thinking that a quantity of loot would be as welcome as the Governor's head and Hausa captives, they desisted from pursuit, and shouldering our valuable stores marched back to their camps around Kumassi. Here Antoa Mensa was questioned as to why he had returned without having carried out the order given to him, and being unable to give a satisfactory answer was degraded from his high position. This Antoa Mensa was a mushroom growth of the rising. Chief of the Kumassi town of Antoa, he had come to the front by the vigour of his espousal of the cause of the rebels. He was an unflinching opponent to British rule, and by his unbending advice at the council of chiefs did more than anyone else to strengthen and consolidate the rebel forces. He brought with him all the young men of his town, and through his influence and example many waverers were induced to throw in their lot

with the malcontents. He was well known to and
hated by a loyal Kumassi chief with us, for he had
seized and appropriated one of his wives.

There were one or two instances of theft of our
goods by our own people. They suspected that
the boxes contained either food or drink, and the
temptation to force them open and satisfy their
cravings was too great to be resisted. Two men
were brought into the village in which we rested
for the night in a dying state. One of them was
clasping in his hand a label taken off a bottle of
Scrubb's ammonia. It was not difficult to discover that actuated by hunger they had broken
a box belonging to one of the officers, containing
among other things a bottle of whisky and a
bottle of Scrubb's ammonia. They had finished
them both.

On this most disastrous march we lost nearly
everything we had. I had only now left to me the
clothes I was wearing. With the exception of
three bottles of whisky all our small supply of stores
which we had with so much care put by for this
terrible march, and held sacred for it, had been
thrown away, and we were now entirely dependent
upon such food as we could find in the villages
through which we passed. Filters had been aban-

doned, and the boxes containing drugs and medical comforts for the sick and wounded thrown into the bush, to be discovered by Antoa Mensa and his party and taken triumphantly back to the rebels round Kumassi! The loss of our filters was especially severe, for now we had to drink the muddy and perhaps polluted water just as it came from the river or stream from which it was taken.

Rain was incessant throughout the day, and the road was in a terrible state. It was with the greatest difficulty that my hammock-men made any progress; they had to be changed every half-hour or so, and often I had to get out and walk in mud and slush ankle deep. I was very weary. The cap on my head was saturated with water, and became so heavy as to be quite a burden. How I managed to stumble along I cannot now, when I look back upon it all, understand. Well, I suppose that in the sheer necessity for it I found strength to persevere and struggle on.

The rebels had cleared everything out of the village, and there was no food to be had. After the experience of the first night the refugees were not permitted to come inside the village, but were required to make their own camp on its confines; we were therefore not crowded as we had been at

Losses in the Bush

Terrebum, and our hut was a trifle larger. The one stretcher bed again arrived, and was faithful to me until Cape Coast was reached, but on this night and often again afterwards it was soaked with rain. One of the officers, hearing that we had no food, very generously gave me a small bottle of bovril which he had been carrying in his pocket. ·This and a few plantains which had been gathered from an adjacent plantation formed our dinner. It was meagre fare, but sufficient to stay the pangs of hunger, and thus enable me to get a little of the much-needed rest.

Early the next morning we were once more on the move, hoping to reach a place called N'kwanta, and there to find a good supply of food for ourselves and for our half-famished troops and carriers, as well as for the refugees who followed the column. N'kwanta is the principal town of the Ashanti tribe of that name. The King of N'kwanta —a fine, courtly old gentleman—I have already referred to as having been with us in Kumassi. He came with other kings to the durbar held on the 28th March, and upon the commencement of the rising was one of the first to hold himself aloof from it, and to express his loyalty to the Queen. When we had to leave Kumassi and take this terrible journey to the coast, he and his followers were with the other loyal kings and chiefs placed in the column, and it was one of his chiefs who acted as our guide. At the taking of the stockade at Patassi the guide was badly wounded, but he made light of it, and did not relinquish his post until he had brought us to N'kwanta.

The rebels fired a few shots at us as we left the village as a kind of farewell, for they troubled us no more. This day's march was, so far as the track itself was concerned, one of the worst, for the road was in a terrible state, and there was a never-ending hill to be climbed. I think the dread of attack was lost sight of in the difficulties of the journey. The hill, which was reached about midday, was at times very steep, so steep that my hammock-men could not carry me up, and there was no alternative but to get out and climb. I thought I should never reach the top of it. Always there was visible what appeared to be the top of the hill, yet when, after much tribulation, I had reached it, I found that it was not the true top, and I had to struggle on again. Rather more than half-way up the hill there was a plateau, on which was a large plantation of plantains and papaws. The papaw is a very excellent product, and is to be found everywhere in the Gold Coast, growing as a tree, the trunk of which is like a gigantic cabbage stalk. At the top are some short green boughs covered with large leaves, and clustering round the tree is the fruit. This is as large as a good-sized vegetable marrow, which in taste it very much resembles when cooked green. The ripe papaw turns a golden tint, and is then a delicious and refreshing fruit; cut in slices with a little lime or lemon juice squeezed on it, it resembles somewhat the musk melon. This plantation was too great a temptation to our men; not only the carriers but even the Hausas, throwing aside discipline, rushed for this El Dorado of food. In a moment, regardless of the consequences, for who could tell whether we were or were not among hostile people, fires were lighted, in which hundreds of plantains were put to roast, while the time was filled up by a general gorge of papaws. A halt had necessarily to be made, and when once more the column moved on it was with considerable difficulty that the men could be induced to start. They revelled in the land of plenty, and were oblivious of danger and the necessity for pushing forward to N'kwanta.

Losses in the Bush

At last the top of the hill was reached, and then was disclosed an abrupt and very steep descent on the other side of it. My heart sank, but N'kwanta had to be reached, and the descent had therefore to be made. The path was so slippery that I had to have a man on either side of me holding my arms in order to prevent my falling. We reached the foot of the hill only to find that we were in an undulating, difficult country, with the road passing either over hills or through swamps and streams where the route was obliterated. One stream I remember well. It was some thirty feet wide and flowing swiftly. Across it was a tree-trunk, over which I saw those in front of me crossing like Blondin on his tight-rope. How was I to get over? I knew that I could not balance myself on this tree-trunk, and that if I tried it I should inevitably fall into the stream below. The difficulty was solved by my cook insisting on carrying me over in his arms. He was a tall man fortunately, and he managed to take me over successfully, but more than once he stumbled, and I thought that I should be dropped into the torrent. Often the road led among high reeds and long grass, which had to be pushed through, and many a time that day I thought we had lost our way, and might suddenly emerge into some unfriendly village, there to be either taken prisoner or shot down.

At last N'kwanta came in sight perched on a hill, up which we had to climb. But what, then, did fatigue matter? We could see the Union Jack flying on a flagstaff in the centre of the town, and the King's people drawn up to receive the Governor, and to welcome back their King. We knew that, although still in Ashanti, we were in a country the people of which were friendly, and that we could rest without fear of attack. A guard of honour of Hausas had been drawn up to salute the Governor on his arrival. Weary and haggard he received the salute, and immediately fell forward in a faint, thoroughly exhausted by the long march and lack of food.

There was to be no lack of food here for our men. On all sides were signs of plenty. Fires were burning everywhere, and the cooking of food was the sole pursuit. Our poor starved Hausas and natives, who had borne their trials and hardships without a murmur, were now at last to take their fill; tinned beef and hard biscuits were things of the past, food to which they were unaccustomed and which they probably never again wished to

Losses in the Bush

see, and once more they had before them the diet in which their hearts delighted. It was a pleasant sight to see the joy with which they welcomed their altered prospects, and the dispersal of the gloom which had for so long rested upon all of us like a pall.

CHAPTER XVI

A WELCOME RESTING-PLACE

BEFORE proceeding further with our own
adventures I will describe the reception
which the King of N'kwanta received from his
people. Quite an old man with hair turned grey
and a white beard, of very quiet and dignified
demeanour, and with a face in which kindliness is.
the principal expression, he is as unlike the usual
run of Ashanti kings as possible. Some distance
before we reached the village we heard drums
beating and horns blowing, which in my nervous
state was very upsetting, although the natives with
us assured me that the drums were playing a
welcome, and that there was nothing to be alarmed
about. It is a well known fact that in West Africa
drum-beating is quite a science. It is the native
method of transmitting information, and, as the
sound of a drum carries a great distance, in this
way communications can be sent from village to
village, and matters made known to the whole tribe
in a marvellously short space of time.

A Welcome Resting-place

The people seemed very delighted to see their King back amongst them, and he was carried up the hill in his native hammock to the flagstaff, followed by the rejoicing and excited people. The drums which had been playing furiously ceased as soon as he left his hammock. He then solemnly shook hands with all the principal chiefs and people assembled around him. This ceremony over, the drums again beat out their welcome. The King sat down upon his tribal stool, his principal chiefs sitting on their stools on either side of him with his court officials, linguists, court criers, and others ranged behind him. For a short time the people danced before him. It seemed to be etiquette from him neither to speak, nor smile, nor in any way to show that he was at all moved by this loyal display on the part of his subjects. He remained stolid, unmoved, and impassive. When he had had enough of it he got into his hammock again, and was carried to the palace.

What a misnomer! The "palace" ordinarily consists of a few huts arranged in the shape of a square, the sides of the huts being open to the centre. The floor of each hut is in Ashanti raised some eighteen inches or two feet from the ground, and consists of hardened clay smoothed

and coloured a dark red. The courtyard is almost always dirty in the extreme, because in it all the household work of preparing the meals of the occupants of the huts takes place; and it is made the receptacle for rubbish of all kinds, broken pots, and every conceivable form of refuse. In the rains the courtyard receives the drippings of the thatched roofs, and becomes a noisome quagmire, for the natives do not take the trouble to drain off the surface water.

Having rested a short time, the King came round to the Governor's hut to see if we were comfortably housed and everything was in order. The comfort consisted of lying on the mud floor of a three-sided hut, the walls of which were of sliced bamboo, through the interstices of which all movements could be seen, and with a thatched roof in which to my horror lizards were chasing each other in all directions. However, we felt that we were now in comparative safety, and our hearts were full of thankfulness for our deliverance from the many perils of the last three trying days; moreover, we were eagerly looking forward to the dinner which was then being prepared, which would be our first real meal since we left Kumassi. The *menu* was soup, roast chicken, and a native root called koko, which when boiled makes a very fair vegetable. Although there was neither salt, nor bread, nor anything in the culinary line that makes food appetising, the meal appeared to us after our long abstinence to be a real banquet. We had no tablecloth or serviettes. Two boxes placed together served well enough as a table, upon which the dishes were placed. Out of a tin cup and a broken claret glass we drank weak whisky and water, our only beverage; and the water, shall I ever forget it? It had been boiled, but unfiltered it still maintained its dark colour and repulsive taste, which not even the whisky could disguise.

It was in N'kwanta that I was able to have the first change of clothing since leaving Kumassi. But what was I to put on? All my spare clothes had been lost on the march, and I was left with only what I was wearing. However, those of the officers with us who had anything at all to spare were very good, and between them all I managed somehow or other. It was always a trying time to me when, at the various stages of the march, I had to relinquish my one set of woman's clothing into the hands of the "washerman," because it meant that they had to be put on damp and draggled when we started the next morning.

A Welcome Resting-place

So weary was every person in the column that it was decided to run the risk of staying two days at N'kwanta, so that all might have a rest and be better able to undertake the wearisome journey that still lay before us. The two wounded officers were also not doing well, and my husband was completely knocked up by the long march on foot, his hammock-men having proved too weak to carry him. Food was difficult to find for so many famished men with ravenous appetites, and the price of it was almost at famine rates, but still there was enough, and I doubt if anyone thought twice of the cost.

CHAPTER XVII

LETTERS AND TELEGRAMS

OUR first day at N'kwanta was a varied one of joy and anxiety. My husband early in the morning had addressed a letter to the officer commanding any relieving force there might be on its way to Kumassi, and had despatched it by the linguists of the King of Bekwai, who had been with us in Kumassi. These men said that there was a bush-path to their country, and that they thought they might manage to elude the enemy and get safely through. The senior linguist, Kofi Yami, was an old acquaintance of my husband; it was he who in the troublous times preceding the expedition to Kumassi under Colonel (now General Sir Francis) Scott in 1896 had come to Accra, bearing protestations of friendship to the Queen from the King of Bekwai, and an assurance that he would not join Prempeh and the tribes who were supporting him. Kofi Yami had had a rough time of it in Kumassi, but that was all over now, and his face was aglow with pleasure at the thought of getting back to his country and his family; so with a present in his hand he left us with a glad heart.

He got through all right, and delivered the letter which explained the action which the beleaguered force in Kumassi had taken in consequence of lack of food, the fact that a force sufficient to guard the fort had been left behind, and that it was absolutely essential that it should be relieved by the 15th of July, up to which date it had been provisioned. The substance of this letter was telegraphed by Colonel Willcocks to the Secretary of State for the Colonies, and an assurance given at the same time that the relieving column then at Esumeja—ten miles distant from Kumassi—would reach the place by that date. Colonel Willcocks' telegram was as follows :—

"FUMSU, *July 4th.*

"Just received letter sent by Governor Hodgson, in which he states that he, with 600 native soldiers, under the command of Major Morris, departed from Coomassie, June 23rd, by way of Patiasa and Terrebum.

"Two British officers severely wounded; does not send names. Captain Bishop, Inspector of

Letters and Telegrams

Constabulary, Gold Coast, and Ralph, Lagos Constabulary, and 100 native soldiers, have been left behind at Coomassie with rations up to July 15th.

"I will personally relieve Coomassie by that date under any circumstances. Hodgson states that he intended to go over River Ofin by way of Mampong to Cape Coast, but I have applied to him by urgent special messengers to leave behind as many men as possible, in order to give assistance to me to enter into Coomassie.

"Burroughs, with 400 native soldiers, arrived at Dompoassi 1st July. Enemy's force taken completely by surprise, stockades evacuated by them. Burroughs captured forty guns, quantity of gunpowder and caps, and also killed thirty of the enemy; our loss one native soldier killed in action, three native soldiers wounded.

"Willcocks."

Simultaneously with the despatch of Kofi Yami and the Bekwais with him, a Hausa runner was sent to Cape Coast with the following telegram to the Secretary of State :—

"Have the honour to inform you that in consequence of column for relief not arriving, and reduction of food supplies to three days and a half, it was necessary to make an attempt to push through rebel forces. Taking two days' supply of rations, and leaving remainder for force of 100 left to guard the fort under Assistant-Inspectors Bishop and Ralph sufficient for twenty-four days, the column, 600 strong, left Coomassie at 5.45 a.m., June 23, under the command of Major Morris, D.S.O., accompanied by 700 carriers, loyal Kings of Mampon, Juabin, Aguna, N'kwanta, and Nsuta, with their followers and all Europeans, inclusive of members of Basel Mission.

"I was able to remain at Coomassie till the 23rd June only by reduction of supply of rations to a minimum. The force was too weak to attempt to break out by the Prahsu road, where the rebel forces were in great numbers, but it was given out that I should take that road, and the rebel forces, hearing this, fortunately remained to await arrival.

"The route decided on after full consideration was that through Patassi and Terrebum to Ekwanta. At Patassi there was a stockade which was captured by a flank movement with loss of one killed and several wounded, including Captains Marshall and Leggett, both severely wounded. At every village passed through the advance guard was attacked and the rearguard harassed, but Terrebum was reached with only loss of six killed and several slightly wounded. Many of the carriers, weakened by hunger, threw away their loads, and nearly all of us have lost clothing and such provisions as we had.

"The march to Ekwanta has been one of great difficulty and privation, the hammock-men being

o

too weak to perform duty, and the column ham-
pered with large numbers of persons who followed
from Coomassie. We are halting here for two
days to recruit, and we hope to reach Cape Coast
in ten days' time. We have had letters sent to
officer commanding column for relief, who, from
what I hear, has reached Bekwai, acquainting him
with situation, and saying that it is absolutely
necessary to relieve fort not later than July 15.
The people encamped round the fort suffered from
starvation terribly, and the rate of mortality was
at the last upwards of thirty per diem. The scenes
witnessed were terrible.

"I could not attack the rebel forces with any
determination, owing to insufficient ammunition,
and we marched out of Coomassie on 23rd June
with only 150 rounds of ammunition per man.
Major Morris arrived at Coomassie with 230
Hausas on the 15th May. His services in these
anxious and trying times have been invaluable to
me; I cannot speak too highly of the way in which
he carried out arrangements for leaving Coomassie.
I have had no news of any kind since the 29th
April, when the Lagos Constabulary reached
Coomassie. Regret to inform you that Middlemist,
Deputy Inspector-General, died of malarious fever
6th May, and Maguire, Assistant Inspector of Con-
stabulary, killed in action 29th May.

"HODGSON."

Letters and Telegrams

The same morning news was brought in that troops under white officers had arrived at Esumeja, and that more were on their way up. It was stated also that they would reach Kumassi the next day, and great was our joy at the thought that those whom we had left behind to guard the flag would so soon be relieved. If only the relief had come earlier!

The question now before us was how we were to get our column across the Ofin River, which was two days' march beyond N'kwanta. It was decided to send a small force to the riverside, with some natives supplied by the King of N'kwanta, to construct rafts, and if possible to commandeer any canoes that could be found. The party moved off early with instructions to be on the alert against attack, and to have two or more rafts ready and in working order by the time of our arrival.

In the afternoon the King sent word to say that he had some important news to communicate. He arrived in our compound with his linguists to announce that people from his outlying villages had come in, and reported that Kumassis had attacked and plundered them, and had in some cases carried off the women and children. Major Morris was sent for, and the matter was gone into. It appeared, from the statements of the people who had reported to the King, that the attack had been made by Kumassis from the Kumassi villages in the country, and not from Kumassi itself. The King seemed to be much agitated and genuinely alarmed, but he was told that the column could not possibly be employed in punishing the offenders.

I think both the Governor and Major Morris had some doubt as to the accuracy of the statements, and had an impression that the King's object was to induce us to rid him of the Kumassis living in his district, the attacks being probably fabricated, the better to effect his object. Anyhow he could not have considered himself to be in very great danger, for when the column left N'kwanta two days later he elected to remain in his country, although a safe convoy to the coast was offered to him. Later he stated that the column was to be attacked by the Ashantis at the Ofin River, but this also fortunately proved to be incorrect. However, the news at the time was very disquieting, and made us wish to be able to push on at once so as not to give the enemy time to concentrate in force. But the Ofin River was in flood, and it would have been useless to reach it until all arrangements for crossing it had been made, for

there were no villages on its banks, and no places therefore where we could encamp and find food.

The whole of the next day we spent in taking stock of ammunition and stores, getting returns of killed and wounded, and seeing exactly what carriers were fit for duty. In the evening the King and his chiefs were assembled and addressed by the Governor, who thanked them for their loyalty to the Queen, and for the good work which the King and those with him had done while in Kumassi. The King was then given a present of money for his services.

CHAPTER XVIII

IN DEEP WATERS

EARLY next morning the column was on the
move, everyone being on the alert against
attack, but the only fight we had on that day and
on many succeeding days was with the swamps
and difficulties which all along the track we had
to encounter. The road was very favourable for
ambuscades, but fortunately for us the Ashantis
held aloof, and we passed on without molestation
from them. Many gymnastic feats were performed
on this and other days, perhaps the worst being
when we had to cross deep streams or small rivers
on a felled tree. My cook was my "handy man"
through all difficulties, and he conducted me across
these crazy and alarming tree bridges with great
care and steadiness. Sometimes, if the stream
was not too deep, he would pick me up in his
arms and carry me over. It required not a little
nerve to embark upon these very dangerous and
slippery crossings, but it is astonishing how when

a thing has to be done it can generally be carried through.

After a wearying day, with rain towards the end of it, we came upon Edubia, the plantation village where we intended to pass the night. It was a picture to make angels weep, but the approach to it was fine and beautiful, had one been in the humour for admiring scenery. Nature in all her silent glory yielded for our use an abundance of well-grown plantain and papaw trees, and others good for food and making glad our hearts. On one side of the road was a hill covered with these trees dipping down into a natural basin; a thin purple-blue mist was rising over everything, making the scene more beautiful, but more deadly for the white man passing through it. To reach the village we had to walk ankle deep in mud. Of course there had been no halt for refreshment during the day, for we were afraid of lingering, and so giving the rebels an opportunity to screw their courage up to attack us.

The first thing I saw on getting in was the Governor sitting on a tree stump under a palm tree, talking to one of the officers, each eating a ripe papaw, and appearing cheerful. Everything looked so dismal, and I was so tired and muddy

In Deep Waters

that I felt quite angry with them for taking such a bright view of things, and would not for a short while allow myself to accept the slice of papaw handed to me on a penknife, although I was famishing. The rain had now become a steady downpour, the huts were too miserable for description, and our two sick officers were very ill indeed. Could anything be more heartbreaking? That night a gun went off, which woke up the camp, and we imagined that the expected attack had really come, but after investigation it was fortunately found to be a false alarm.

Next morning we left the village, having first laid to rest Captain Marshall, who, to the very great grief of all, had passed away. Poor fellow! a more cheery, gallant officer there could not be. Everyone liked him, and it was inexpressibly sad to think that we had to leave him lying in the quiet forest far from all those he loved.

Another long and weary march brought us to a similar village, where we spent the night, having the added sorrow before leaving it of burying our other dear officer, Captain Leggett. He had been in every engagement since the very beginning of the rebellion, and was wounded each time, but only once severely enough to confine him to bed. A most energetic man, he was always doing work nobly for others, and never thinking of himself. The death of these two officers cast a gloom and sadness over all; but on and on we had to go, for we were not yet out of Ashanti-land, and until we crossed the Ofin River we dared not consider ourselves safe.

The crossing of this river was a great undertaking. Before reaching it we had to wade through a swamp, in parts more than four feet deep. This took us two hours. The soldiers carried their coats, holding them aloft with their arms and ammunition pouches on their heads, so as to keep them out of the water. Not a sign of a path anywhere was to be seen, nothing but this pea-soup-looking water on all sides. Short men had a bad time, for the water went almost over their heads, and it was so cold that teeth were chattering loudly. Every now and then there would be a great splash, when some unfortunate carrier, missing his footing or treading on a hidden snag, over-balanced himself and hurled his load into the water and probably himself too; then he would dive under and bring the dripping box to view again. It was in a way amusing, but at the same time very annoying to the owner of the box.

In Deep Waters

During all the wading through the water my bearers were fortunately able to carry me in my hammock. It was a very difficult and tiring task for them. Often had they to hold up my hammock at arm's length so as to clear the water; but although I had men on either side to place their arms under the hammock in order to lift it in the more difficult places, it happened more than once that it dipped, and I found myself lying in a pool. But this was better than having to wade, for even if I could have survived I am sure that my one suit of clothes could not. I found it very difficult to keep from falling out of the hammock, as the side men constantly gave it a tilt which precipitated me to the very edge, and I only saved myself by clutching at the pole.

In front walked a guide with a long stick probing for holes and snags. At the end of two hours we found ourselves on the river-bank. Here we came upon a mixed crowd of Hausas and carriers, all gesticulating at the top of their voices. It was a strange sight. Right in front of us was the trunk of an enormous tree which had been felled in order to serve as a bridge, and upon this trunk were seated Hausas with their guns and carriers with their loads, making no attempt as

In Deep Waters

far as we could see to move on. In the water around the tree-trunk were many others up to their necks in the stream. The cause of the stoppage was soon revealed. The tree-trunk fell short of the bank by some twenty feet, and the intervening space was some seven feet deep in water. The trunk was very slippery, and the work of getting along it resembled very much that of contests on a greasy pole. I watched the men warily moving along. A Hausa somewhat more brisk than cautious at once paid the penalty for his temerity, and overbalancing himself fell backwards into the water. Clutching his carbine he emerged spluttering and breathless, the crowd jeering and laughing heartily as if they themselves were in no similar danger of a ducking.

By this time the Governor had reached the tree and clambered up, and from this vantage point directed the crossing, so that in about half an hour my hammock-men were able to move on. But how was I to reach the bank? My bearers could do nothing more, for the water was too deep for them to carry me further, and I could not swim. Suddenly my husband, who was still sitting astride the tree, called out to me that a canoe was coming. It had been sent up to assist us in crossing over the deep pool. This was a great relief to me, but to get into a canoe from a hammock is a feat not easy of accomplishment. The chances are that you land anywhere but in the canoe. However, I managed it somehow, and thought myself exceptionally lucky. The canoe had three or four inches of water in it, but a biscuit tin had been placed for me to sit upon, and as I was already fairly wet through I did not think much about it.

The canoe had been brought up by a Hausa sergeant, with instructions to take us over the pool to the river-bank, down which we were to walk until we came to the place where the rafts were at work. The message the man gave us was that we were to pass down the river in the canoe, a mistake on his part which nearly cost us our lives. Having crossed the pool we found ourselves very close to the river, which was easily accessible, as the bank was sufficiently submerged to admit of the canoe being punted over it. In the middle of the canoe in a pool of water sat the Governor. I was before him on my biscuit tin, and behind were my cook and the Hausa sergeant. The latter had the steering paddle in his hand, but fortunately for us my cook asked him if he could steer, and

NATIVE DRUMMERS

In Deep Waters

finding that he knew very little about it took the paddle and his place. Now the cook, like all natives of Accra, was quite at home in a canoe, and the sergeant was told to sit down and keep quiet, for he was inclined to resent his displacement. Things being thus adjusted, we made for the river, which, to my terror, I found a swirling torrent moving at racing speed. It was too late to turn back. We were caught in the current and hurled along at a tremendous pace. My cook Henry kept the canoe steady, and all appeared to be going well, when suddenly we landed on a snag, which in a moment turned us broadside to the stream. The canoe tilted over and began to fill, but righted itself upon our throwing by natural impulse the weight of our bodies to the opposite side. Still, there we were stuck in mid-stream, and broadside on. It seemed as if nothing could save us. The Hausa sergeant lost his head, and made an effort to start up, apparently to throw himself out of the canoe and swim for it, but upon being shouted at to remain quiet he fortunately relapsed into his place. Henry was now working away with his paddle, and my husband, who was nearest to the snag, was cautiously assisting by pulling the canoe gradually forward. Then it moved slightly, and at last we were clear. I doubt if death had ever been nearer than when we were on that snag.

Off we went again at racing speed, but had not gone more than a few yards when we dashed into the branches of a mimosa tree which had fallen rather more than half-way across the river. I had my back to it and knew nothing of the danger until I found myself crashing into the branches and nearly lifted out of the canoe. The thorny branches twisted themselves into my hair. To struggle would have resulted in upsetting the canoe. I yelled to Henry to hold up the canoe, but the current was too strong. Instinct made me put my hands up and grasp the branch. I used all my force to break it. Fortunately it was an old one and yielded to my efforts, and the canoe passed through, my hair torn and my hands bleeding from the thorns they had encountered. There was no time to think of pain, for on we sped on our mad career. At last we heard voices in the distance, and knew that we must be nearing the crossing-place. Soon the rafts came in sight, but here another danger awaited us, because across the river ropes had been fixed for the purpose of working the rafts, and if by any chance we were to crash into them the canoe would most certainly be upset. But this time Henry was equal to the occasion, for as we neared the ropes he brought the canoe broadside to them, so that we were able to grasp one of them and work ourselves to the bank.

CHAPTER XIX

A DAY OF SAFETY DAWNS

IT was with very thankful hearts that, stepping ashore, we found ourselves once more in the Colony, and with the river between us and Ashanti. It was now past three o'clock : we had had nothing to eat since early morning, and were very hungry. The biscuit tin which had been my seat in the canoe was opened, and from it was produced all the food we had, namely some very insipid cold boiled mutton and fresh maize. Now, Indian corn when eaten with hot butter at a well-appointed luncheon-table appeals to me greatly; but cold, after having been boiled in muddy water, it is quite another matter. Hunger, however, overcomes many scruples, and I have no doubt that I made a good meal.

The rafts, two of them, were hard at work taking the Hausa troops as well as the carriers and their loads over the river, and this was where we should have crossed it, a distance of forty yards, instead of wildly risking our lives in that mad rush down stream. The process was a slow one, and the loads were saturated; but still it was a grand thing to be clear of the enemy, and to feel that we were really safe, for it was now fairly certain that we should not be attacked or followed by the rebels.

The village we were to stay the night at was another plantation one, and about an hour's march from the river. The way was pitted with gold holes—great yawning caverns, to fall down which would be almost certain death. They zigzagged on either side of the narrow path. This was not the first time we had encountered such terrors, but these particular gold holes were impressed upon my mind by my hammock-men dropping me across one. The front man fell down, away went the hammock, but fortunately it fell straight and not on the tilt, or I should assuredly have been shot down the gold hole. Gold is good, and possibly I have never been so near to its source before, but I would rather be without a fortune than find it by being shot to the bottom of one of these holes. That same afternoon one of the carriers actually fell into one, and his comrades had to haul him out with ropes.

A Day of Safety Dawns

That evening we had a great treat, and after our
adventurous day one much appreciated. One of
our servants, with many smiles, produced a small
bottle of champagne which he had managed to
acquire either at Kumassi or elsewhere, and had
carried all this distance. He evidently thought
that having now left the enemy's country behind us,
the event was one which ought to be commemorated,
and I suppose he also knew that no inquiries would
be made as to how or where he had procured the
precious bottle. I must confess that we thoroughly
enjoyed the spoil, and asked no questions.

Next morning we moved on to the first real
village met with since leaving N'kwanta, where
the people—Denkeras—were not only of course
friendly, but very glad to welcome us. Food was
plentiful, but the prices exorbitant. It had been
necessary, in order to avoid delay, to break up the
column, as it was impossible to take such a large
number of people over in one day, and it had been
decided that after crossing the Ofin River the
column should move onwards to the coast in two
parties at a day's interval. Major Morris was in
command of the first party, with which the Governor
travelled; and Captain Aplin, Inspector-General of
the Lagos Hausas, of the second. The Governor

A FETISH GROVE

Face page 270

A Day of Safety Dawns

was anxious to push on to Cape Coast as quickly as possible, in order to ascertain what was being done for the relief of Kumassi, for it must not be forgotten that since the 29th of April no authentic news of any kind had reached us from the outside world. We had only had rumours brought into us by our native spies, who could not be depended upon. From this village—Akwabosu—the following telegram was sent to the Secretary of State for the Colonies :—

"AKWABOSU, 1st *July*.

"Crossed Ofin River 30th June and 1st July. Following Europeans left Coomassie with force: Governor of Gold Coast, Lady Hodgson, Commissioner and Commandant Morris, Special Service Officers Marshall and Digan, Inspector-General Aplin, Travelling Commissioner Armitage, Inspector Parmeter, Assistant Inspectors Leggett and Berthon, Gold Coast Constabulary, and Cochrane and Read, Lagos Constabulary; Medical Officers Garland, Chalmers, Tweedy, Graham, Gold Coast Colony, and Macfarlane of Lagos; Telegraph Clerk-in-charge Branch; Members of Basel Mission, namely, two Ramseyer, two Jost, two Haasis, Weller, last-named dangerously ill; David and Grundy of Ashanti Company.

"Regret to inform you of death from wounds of Marshall, Leggett, former 28th June, latter 29th

273

A Day of Safety Dawns

June. Passage across Ofin River very difficult owing to floods. Hardships of journey from Coomassie have been very severe. Most of the severely wounded Hausas have since died; others are missing. In addition to officers mentioned in previous telegrams as left in charge of fort add name of Hay, Medical Officer. "HODGSON."

The messenger sent with this telegram took also telegrams from the several European officers to their friends. It seemed such a joy once again to be in touch with home, and to feel what happiness the few words we were sending, as winged messengers, would bring to those anxious ones who had watched and waited so many weary weeks for news of us. But there were two homes to be saddened by the news, and my thoughts often turned towards those whom the cruel hand of death had robbed, and my sympathies were with them in their grief and sorrow.

One little excitement we had at Akwabosu was the making out a list of stores to be sent up to us from Cape Coast—tea, sugar, milk, butter, salt, and so forth. How we looked forward to meeting these things on our way down. This may sound very greedy, but to be without everything, with no salt even to add to the boiled and insipid food which formed our everyday unvaried meal, more than justified our longings.

We had now to travel through a monotonous country, the road leading always through the silent and unchanging forest. There were streams to cross, swamps to wade through, gigantic trees to crawl under or to pass round by struggling through the jungle, but always the silent forest, black in its density, and with never a sign of life in it. This damp, dismal, and impenetrable jungle was terribly nerve-shaking. The excitement which had given me courage while in Ashanti was gone, and each day I felt as if I could never win to the end of the journey, and that I must after all give in. Our progress was very slow. Each day we travelled for ten hours, but sometimes, nay often, we scarcely did more than a mile an hour, so many swamps impeded us and so difficult was the road.

News in West Africa travels quickly among the natives, and whenever we passed through a village they were sitting outside their houses or watching at their doors to see us pass. Everywhere were signs of loyalty and pity, the chiefs greeting the Governor with every mark of respect, and sending him, in accordance with native custom, presents of sheep or fowls or roots. At every village cooked

A Day of Safety Dawns

food and fresh water had been prepared for the
Hausas and carriers, and were distributed to them
as we passed through. The amount that a native
can eat during the day is absolutely astonishing,
and I could not have believed it had I not seen it
with my own eyes. One of my hammock-men in
particular never ceased to eat, and his greediness
even called down upon his head the rebukes of his
fellow-bearers, not, however, I am afraid, because he
was greedy, but because they found him unable to
do his share of the work.

One of our halting-places for the night was a
large village called Dengiassi. It is situated in the
district of Tchuful, and was founded by an Ashanti
tribe of that name which had migrated from Ashanti
about the year 1885. There is still a district in
Ashanti called Dengiassi, and in fact in our march
we passed through a corner of it. The tribe finding
itself at loggerheads with the all-powerful Kumassis
decided, in order to avoid defeat and slavery, to
migrate. They sent messengers to the Governor
of the Gold Coast begging permission to cross the
Ofin River. This was granted, the King of
Tchuful at the Governor's request having promised
them an asylum in the uninhabited part of his
country in which they are now located. Here they

cleared the forest, and built for themselves an enormous and thriving town, calling it after the name of the tribe.

It was strange to find oneself once more among Ashantis. The chief is, however, a very loyal man, and had the Union Jack flying on a staff in front of his house. Part of his house he had made ready for the Governor's occupation, and we had hardly seated ourselves in our quarters when the noise of tom-toms and the blowing of horns announced the arrival of the chief and his court. He was a fine broad-shouldered man, and although every inch an Ashanti was quick to express his loyalty to the Queen and friendship for the Governor. He brought many presents— sheep, fowls, eggs, and root-crops—and in a long speech stated how pleased he was to find that the Governor had eluded his enemies and arrived in the Colony. Throughout our stay in Dengiassi he was most attentive, and he was careful to be present and to wish us *bon voyage* when we left in the morning.

From Dengiassi we had to journey through the forest, and I shall never forget the weariness of that day. There was not a sign of life of any kind—not even the stir of a leaf by a passing breeze, absolutely nothing to break the deadly stillness of the forest. Even the native hammock-men, who always chatter among themselves, plodded on in silence, and with slackened step seemed to have fallen victims to the tyranny of the situation, and merged their identity in the general lassitude. For more than ten hours we wandered on, and when at length we reached the small village where the halt for the night was to be made I fairly succumbed from exhaustion.

After this day villages were more frequent, and at last we reached Mampon, the chief town of the district of Tchuful, and the residence of the king of the tribe of that name. I was not impressed with the King, who, although thoroughly loyal and anxious to show his loyalty, seemed to be unable to command the respect of his chiefs and linguists, for during his conversation with the Governor he was more than once corrected by one or other of them, and his short, querulous replies to these interruptions were evidently distasteful and received in bad part. He was exceedingly anxious to obtain guns and gunpowder for his people from the Government, so that he might lead them against the Ashantis; but the Governor felt that the possession of warlike stores, always

LOYAL KING OF MAMPON (ASHANTI)

Face page 278

A Day of Safety Dawns

coveted acquisitions by the natives, was more dominant in the King's mind than the desire to fight, and, as he was not then aware of the steps which were being taken for the subjugation of the Ashantis, returned an equivocal answer, telling the King to send messengers to the coast with him, whence he would let him know whether his men would be armed or employed as carriers. The fear of the latter alternative probably deterred the King from sending messengers, for they neither came with us nor followed, so far as I know, subsequently.

At Mampon both my husband and I, worn out by the fatigues and hardships of the journey, were prostrated with fever. The doctors insisted on our remaining there until the fever abated, so there was nothing for it but to obey. My husband arranged, however, that Major Morris and the main body of the Hausas should push on to Cape Coast, as he could not feel sure that the letter which he had sent from N'kwanta to the officer commanding the relief column would have reached its destination, and as it was absolutely necessary that no time should be lost in effecting the relief of the garrison left behind in Kumassi to guard the fort.

A Day of Safety Dawns

It was only a few hours after Major Morris had left that a letter written in French arrived from Colonel Wilkinson, who it then appeared was in command of the advance guard of the relief column. This letter contained the first authentic news which the Governor had received since the 29th April, and although it told him plainly that a column was on its way up, it did not inspire hope that it would reach Kumassi by the 15th July. The letter had been intended for delivery at N'kwanta, but we had left before the messenger arrived there, and so he had followed on with it. But for the fact that we had been delayed by fever it could not have reached us before we arrived at Cape Coast. A request was made in the letter that all available Hausas should be sent from N'kwanta to Esumeja, and I remember saying to my husband, "well, how did they expect us to be able to convoy the missionaries, loyal kings and chiefs, carriers, and, in fact, all the party safely out of Ashanti if we were deprived of all our troops, and why could they not have reversed the position, and hurried up with their available troops to our relief at Kumassi?" When I made this remark we did not know, as we learnt subsequently, that one of the many letters which my

A Day of Safety Dawns

husband had sent from the fort, written in French, saying that the provisions could only last until the 23rd June, had safely passed through the rebel lines and been delivered. As all the world knows, the fort was relieved on the 15th July, and to me it seems strange that, as the situation at Kumassi was known to the officer commanding the relief column, operations were not hurried on, and the difficulties due to weather, the state of the roads, and fatigue overcome at once, as they were overcome three weeks later, when the troops forming the relief column were moved up at a rate quite unknown to the column since its formation. Why was there so long a halt on the part of the column at Prahsu, which is certainly not the most pleasant of places to spend a fortnight at? It was said that the delay was due to waiting for a gun, which after all was not employed in raising the siege; but I am not sure of the authenticity of this statement, for my husband would never talk to me about important official matters, nor would he satisfy my natural curiosity.

CHAPTER XX

THE JOY OF REACHING HOME

WE were now within two days' march of Cape Coast. Jukwa, the residence of the King of Denkera, was our next halting-place. Much to our disappointment we had not received any of the stores for which we had sent a messenger to Cape Coast, but in our journey to Jukwa we met Captain Durham Hall, one of the Assistant Commissioners of the Gold Coast Police, and another officer, accompanied by a large number of armed Denkeras, on their way to join the expeditionary force under Colonel Willcocks. Captain Hall was most kind, and I shall never forget the pleasure I had in once more drinking a cup of tea, eating some good English biscuits, and hearing news of the outside world.

The Denkeras seemed to be very pleased at meeting the Governor, and King Inkwauta Bissa, whom we met covered with gold ornaments, came out of the palanquin in which he was being carried

and greeted him with every demonstration of pleasure. They had often met before, and were old
friends. The Denkeras in the meantime were
firing off their new guns to express their gratifica-
tion, and I was very glad when, after my husband
had wished good luck to the King, the order was
given to them to move on. They were in no sort
of formation, and I wondered whether they would
prove useful when they came in contact with the
enemy.

Jukwa, when we reached it, proved to be a very
wretched place, and the house in which we stayed,
although a pretentious one with two storeys, was
dirty and dilapidated. It was evidently a town
which had seen better days, but had dwindled in
importance. Inquiring as to the cause of this, I
learnt that the King hardly ever lived there, but
was nearly always to be found in Cape Coast, the
attractions of town life being more to his taste
than the humdrum of his own village. It can
hardly be a satisfactory arrangement for the Denkera tribe, but he is not the only absentee king,
for now that money is to be made by the grant
of gold concessions many chiefs constantly come
to the Coast with a view to the disposal of
auriferous areas of their tribal lands.

The Joy of Reaching Home ·

At the village where we halted at midday on our way to Jukwa our stores from Cape Coast arrived, and they were the more welcome as it had been raining all day, and we were wet through and miserable. We were now saying good-bye to the forest belt, for the country was almost free from trees and undergrowth, and we could already feel cool, refreshing breezes blowing up from the sea.

Our last day's march, 12th July, was along an excellent road which had been constructed by Government. We received very kindly greetings at all the villages through which we passed, and at last came in sight of Cape Coast and the sea. I was thoroughly and completely worn out, but I knew now that my troubles were nearly at an end, and so took heart again. Outside Cape Coast we were met by a detachment of Gold Coast Police, looking very smart by the side of our dilapidated party, and with them as an escort we made our way to Cape Coast. Here we found the streets crowded with people, many of the women clapping their hands and calling out to us in their native language "welcome! welcome!" One black gentleman ran by the side of my hammock exclaiming "oh, what a trouble, what a trouble you have had!

The Joy of Reaching Home

Welcome! welcome!" At last Government House was reached, and here we found most of the Government officials and the Base Commandant of the Expeditionary Force, who gave me his arm into the house. I could hardly walk or speak, so weak had I become, and I think, too, I was unnerved by all the kindness and sympathy which was being shown to us. One of the nursing sisters was there to help me, and I did so enjoy dressing myself in clothes which she had most thoughtfully and good-naturedly sent to the house, knowing that I had lost all my own. During the afternoon the captain of H.M.S. *Dwarf*, then lying off Cape Coast, signalled to say that he would take the Governor and his party to Accra; and so arrangements were made to proceed on board at eight o'clock the next morning.

Punctually at that hour we left the beach, the officials and a large number of the people being present to witness our departure. What a pleasant time we had on board the *Dwarf!* The captain and officers were so kind and sympathetic, and I cannot soon forget the comfort of lying on deck in an easy-chair, having every care and attention, and drinking in the sea air, which had been so missed in our sojourn up-country.

The Joy of Reaching Home

The welcome we received at Accra was indeed a warm one; the streets were decorated, and bunting was everywhere displayed. As the surf boat grounded a loud cheer rang out, and friends pushed forward to grasp our hands and be the first to speak words of welcome and sympathy. I was carried from the surf boat in a very dilapidated state, for the surf had been a bad one, and my nerves when coming through it had been still worse; but I was placed in Mr. Yates' comfortable carriage, which he had with great kindness driven on to the sand to save my having to walk to the road, and by him driven to Government House. The joy of at last reaching home again will never be forgotten. It was indeed home, and everyone knows the meaning of that word after many wanderings, and such adventures as had befallen us.

Our reception at Accra was cabled to England by Reuter's agent in the following telegram:—

"ACCRA, *July* 12th.

"Sir Frederic and Lady Hodgson and suite arrived here last evening from Cape Coast Castle on H.M. Gunboat *Dwarf*, and met with an extremely cordial reception from the inhabitants and officials."

KINGS OF ACCRA AND CHRISTIANSBORG AWAITING LADY HODGSON

Face page 288

The Joy of Reaching Home

Our troubles were not yet ended, for very soon it was found that all who had been through that terrible time were to pay the penalty now that the excitement and necessity of enduring hardships were over. The strain had been too severe, and the West African climate claimed its due. We went down one after the other with fever, most of the officers being invalided from Cape Coast, and those that came on with us to Accra had sooner or later to follow them.

Great was the excitement when the sick and wounded Hausas landed at Accra, people cheering and escorting them out of the town; and right well did they deserve this demonstration, for no troops could have done their duty better amid trials and hardships as severe as any that have ever had to be borne.

Before leaving for England the Governor held a parade, and publicly thanked the troops for the way they had done their work, sympathising with them over their wounds and the loss of their comrades fallen in battle.

The Hausa cantonments are on a fine site some four miles from Accra, with which they are connected by telephone, so that the Hausas can be brought in quickly on an emergency. The

The Joy of Reaching Home

officers' quarters are quite palatial for West Africa,
and the officers themselves have some little amusement in shooting, as the country about there holds
bush fowl, partridges, and other wild birds, all
excellent eating, and a very grateful change
from the usual everyday routine of chicken and
mutton.

The loyal kings and chiefs now began to arrive,
evidently delighted to be on a visit to the coast.
They were the guests of the Government, and they
deserved to be well treated for their loyalty to
the Queen and the real help they had been at
Kumassi with their fighting men. Our old friend
the King of Aguna was still a thirsty soul, and
would pay me morning visits and send in polite
messages that claret was a nice drink on a hot
morning. He was much struck with Government
House, and signified his intention of building one
like it on his return to his country. I am afraid
his castle will be always only in the air. During
one of his visits he took a great fancy to a little
brass Indian cart and horse that I had on a table;
he insisted on taking it up and running it up and
down the floor with great glee, and when I
presented it to him his delight was quite that of
a child over a new toy. It is not etiquette for a

The Joy of Reaching Home

king to hold or carry anything, so this precious
present was handed over to one of his chiefs;
but the King looked at it with sad eyes as he
parted from it, and once again before leaving the
room ran it up and down the floor.

Shortly before leaving for England we gave a
garden party to the loyal kings and chiefs—loyalties
I called them—and invited the Kings of Christianborg, Jamestown, and Accra to meet them as well
as all the European community. It was a great
success, and quite an interesting event. Invited
with each king were six followers and with each
chief four. A number of interpreters were also
present, so that the guests could converse easily with
the Europeans and others. The kings and chiefs
wore their most gaudy robes, and all the gold
ornaments they had brought away with them from
Kumassi. Hand-shaking is a very important
function with a native, and it was fairly hard work
receiving our guests, and finding some pleasant
remark for each one on his arrival. Tennis and
croquet were played, and great interest was taken
in the games by the loyalties who stood and
watched them. The kings were very dignified
over the refreshments, but many a laughable scene
was enacted by their followers, who brought from

some concealed place a cloth into which dishes of cakes, etc., were bodily emptied, to be stealthily hidden, doubtless for the use of their royal masters later on. During the afternoon the kings and chiefs with their followers were grouped, a picture was taken of them by one of the local photographers, and each king and chief in due time received a copy.

I cannot refrain from mentioning the heroic way in which Mrs. Ramseyer and the two Basel missionary ladies with her bore their trials and hardships during the siege and the march from Kumassi. Mrs. Ramseyer is a lady who, with her husband, has seen many vicissitudes in life. She is now partially paralysed, but throughout she was always resigned to every misfortune—and there were many of them—as it came. Her life was an example to all of us.

On their arrival at Accra, a few days after our own, I went to see Mrs. Ramseyer, and found her comfortably installed at the Basel Mission House, and preparing to move on to their mission station at Aburi, where they intended to stay for a few weeks before they started for Germany. When provisions ran short during the siege we had supplied them as well as we were able, and we did what we could for them while shut up in the fort.

The following is an extract from a letter which Mrs. Ramseyer sent to me as I was leaving Accra :—

"Our Dr. Fisch has taken a little photo of our party. Will you please accept a copy, and think sometimes of us, as we shall always think with gratefulness of you during our memorable stay in the fort. Good-bye, dear Lady Hodgson. Many, many thanks for your great goodness to us. God bless you and His Excellency for it.

"Your grateful

"ROSE RAMSEYER."

At last, on the 29th August, the time had come to leave Accra for England, and, as I was subsequently to learn, for good. Again we were the recipients of a most hearty demonstration. Natives and Mohammedans, all were present to wish us good-bye. The kindly sympathy which had been shown to us by all classes had done much to drive away the recollection of all we had passed through, and now as we made our way through the surf to the s.s. *Fantee*, which was to carry us to England, I felt that I was parting with many friends whose

The Joy of Reaching Home

genuine kindliness to my husband and myself it would be difficult to equal. For the Gold Coast, with all its drawbacks and disadvantages, I shall always have a warm corner in my heart.

CHAPTER XXI

GOLD IN THE GOLD COAST

DURING our journey from Kumassi it was impossible not to notice the extraordinary diligence of the natives in digging for gold. In the Atchina country, in which the Kumassis have their bush villages, and in N'kwanta, right up to the Ofin River, there were abundant signs of the auriferous character of the soil. Pits, often some thirty or forty feet deep, abounded, and as they were commonly dug out upon the line of pathway it was at times difficult for my hammock-men to get along. I am sure that it would be impossible to traverse the road in safety after dark, and more than once I wondered what would happen if we should fail to reach our destination for the night before darkness came on. As a rule the pits are not of greater diameter than will allow a native to descend by placing his back against the circular wall and his feet in notches cut in the walls on the opposite side ; but many that I saw must have been too wide to admit of this primitive method, and native ladders made of bamboos must have been used. I think the pits were more numerous in N'kwanta than elsewhere, but in the neighbourhood of the Ofin River, and in fact until we had left Upper Denkera, which lies within the Colony and to the south of that river, they were to be met with at every turn.

All along the road also there were many indications of quartz reef cropping out above the soil, but apparently the native did not know how to tackle quartz, as all the pits I saw were at a distance from the reefs, and had been sunk in the soft alluvial soil. Once or twice, when crossing over a stream, there appeared to be indications of quartz having been crushed, but I could not ascertain whether this had been done by natives, or by European prospectors in search of concessions.

Notwithstanding the primitive method employed by the natives in obtaining gold, they manage to get a large quantity of it, and must often come across rich pockets, for I have been shown many large nuggets obtained by them. Every Ashanti king and chief is the possessor of gold ornaments, and the regalia attached to each tribal stool is very valuable; even the handles of the swords of office are covered with beaten gold, affixed with gold rivets. The heads of the state umbrellas are generally covered with beaten gold, and one which I saw in the shape of a large bird with its head turned round and pecking its tail must have been covered with at least £15 worth of beaten gold. One of the ornaments of the loyal King of Aguna was a solid gold bracelet, which he valued at £50. At the commencement of the march from Kumassi he found himself without money to buy food for himself and his followers, and £30 was advanced to him, the bracelet being taken as security for the debt. On reaching Accra the bracelet was found to be worth £45, so that the King was not far out in his valuation.

The only place in which Europeans have mined for gold until quite recently, when the enterprise of Mr. E. A. Cade, of the Ashanti Goldfields Corporation, revealed the extraordinary wealth of gold in Ashanti, has been in the district of Wassaw, but almost everywhere gold exists—in Akim, Sefwki, Aowin, Kwahu, the back of Winneba, and Dixcove. The difficulty in the past has been with regard to transport. · The absence of railways and proper roads has locked up the country against all enterprise—machinery had to be sent out cut up into sections weighing not more than could be conveyed by four men when slung on bamboo poles—say two hundredweight. The cost of transport has swallowed up the profits, but all this is to be altered. Already a railway from the coast to the mines in the Taskwa district of Wassaw, a distance of forty miles, is nearing completion, and it is to be carried on at once to Kumassi, in order to assist in the development of the wealth of that country. Less than two years ago the Secretary of State for the Colonies, speaking in the House of Commons in connection with his great work of developing the resources of England's colonial possessions, said, with regard to the Gold Coast: "The Committee may think I have been too sanguine in the past, but I am more confident than ever that these Colonies will turn out to be a most valuable possession, and acting on that belief I am placing on the Colony a certain burden in the shape of debt, with the fullest confidence that before very long it will be able to repay it. I base that not on the consumption of spirits, but upon the general increase in trade which is taking place, and which I anticipate will develop to an extraordinary degree as soon as we get railway communication—this has already been commenced—and also upon the prospects of the gold industry of the country. I confess that I do not wish to boom that industry at this time, but from all the information I have obtained it is going to be, I believe, a most solid, valuable, and profitable industry in the Gold Coast Colony."

Into the Akim district the Government is constructing a good road. It has been completed as far as Sansami, and before I left Accra in August a contract had, I understand, been made with the Goldfields of Eastern Akim Company for the continuation of the road to Apedjua. Eventually, I suppose, a light line of rails will be laid along this road. The companies who are mining in and around Keyneon Kor at the back of Dixcove intend to construct a light line of railway from that place to the field of operations, and thus another rich auriferous district will be opened up. In the case of Aowin, probably the Tano River will afford a fair means of communication. Already private enterprise in connection with the timber industry has done something for this western district by a railway from Half Assinie on the coast to the Uani Lagoon, which is crossed by

means of a steam launch, and access to the Tano
River has been obtained by a canal which has been
dug across the intervening land. In this way the
logs of mahogany, the bulk of which formerly made
their way down the Tano to the French town of
Assinie, are now intercepted at the canal mouth,
and brought to the coast by the shorter route
through the Uani Lagoon.

In order to show the general richness of the
country in gold I will relate what I saw done at
Axim. I was told that gold could be picked up
in the streets. Of course I was incredulous, and
regarded the remark as only a figure of speech.
My informant asseverated that what he said was
quite true, and calling up the sergeant of police—
I was staying at the time in the fort—he asked
him if his wife would go out into the main street
and gather up a bucketful of what we should
call road-scrapings, bring it into the fort, and work
it for gold dust. The woman was summoned, and
it was explained to her what she had to do. In
ten minutes she returned with two galvanised-iron
buckets, one filled with road-scrapings and the
other with water. She brought also some three
or four wooden platters, varying in size from a
large plate to a saucer. She lost no time. Taking

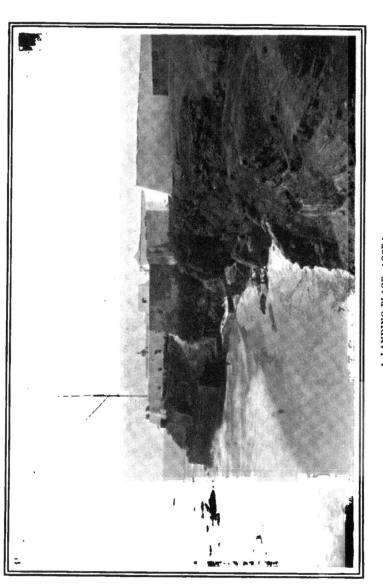

A LANDING-PLACE, ACCRA

Face page 304

out several handfuls of the road - scrapings and
placing them in the largest platter, she picked out
and threw aside the large stones and pebbles, bits
of stick and so forth which were in them, and
loosened the remainder by sprinkling it with water
from the other bucket. This enabled her to remove further refuse. The residuum was put into
the next-sized platter, and the process was repeated
until there was a good quantity of stuff ready in
it for treatment. Taking it up she sprinkled it
freely with water, and by a deft circular movement
of the platter brought the small gravel outwards
which was then thrust off the edge. Two or three
operations of this kind having been gone through,
the stuff, which now looked more like mud than
anything else, was ready for treatment in a smaller
platter. Here the same circular movements were
adopted, and further unpropitious elements were
discarded. Finally the small saucer-shaped platter
was resorted to. The stuff had now resolved itself
into nothing more than a small quantity of black
sand. This was very carefully washed and equally
carefully sifted by similar circular movements, when
at last a final movement brought the sand into the
shape of a crescent on the platter, and to my
astonishment there appeared on its outer edge a

thin gold rim. It was unmistakable. There was
the gold sure enough, and I had to confess that
I was incredulous no longer. The whole operation
took about half an hour, and the result was about
a shilling's worth of gold dust. It seemed to me
that it would be profitable to employ a dozen
women or so to work road-scrapings at so much
a day.

The native method of working the gold pits
for gold is very well described by the late
Mr. G. E. Ferguson — a native Government
officer, who was sent on a mission into Akim
and Kwahu and reported on it upon his return.
He writes :—

"A native miner has but few implements: a
long-bladed spud or digger, a wooden bucket for
baling out the water or hoisting up the stuff, and
a bowl for washing or 'vanning' make up the
list. These and his method of descending his
shaft are shown in the sketch annexed. He rarely
makes his shaft more than three feet in diameter.
Planting one end of his digger into a recess in the
shaft he places the other end diagonally against the
side of the shaft, and supporting himself by it, his
foot is placed in another of the recesses. He then
lengthens out his body and fixes his back firmly
against the side of the shaft. Thus supported,

he removes the digger, plants it in another recess below the first, and by repeating the operation gets to the bottom of the shaft. A tunnel, which cannot be long, for his neighbour's shaft is only fifteen to twenty feet from him, is next driven.

"In some cases there is a quick return—nuggets worth £100 not being rare, as I was informed by the chief of Esiakwa. From all I can learn the yield is about £2 10s. per ton.

"Whatever the yield may be, the numerous shafts serve as catch-pits for surface water, and as the rainy season sets in all the workings are suspended; a few are renewed during the dry season, while most of them are permanently deserted and new shafts sunk. In this way the Akim miner honeycombs the ground, and by interfering with the natural distribution of the water wastes the mineral resources of his country."

There can be no doubt that gold exists in large quantities on the Gold Coast. The whole of the past history of that country is in favour of it, but the question of climate arises when Europeans are employed in mining for it. The climate is undoubtedly bad, but medical science is at work, and the conditions of life on the coast are fast improving. Care must be taken to select men who are not only perfectly sober, but also of strong and sound constitution. Then it is essential that there should be good quarters provided, on sanitary sites, away from native villages; and all Europeans must be provided with good food, of which fresh meat and vegetables should form an important part. If mining companies will adopt these precautions much will have been done towards success.

CHAPTER XXII

LIFE IN WEST AFRICA

A WOMAN'S life on the Gold Coast is not relieved by much variety, although if she is resourceful the days can be made to pass happily, and even the very monotony of life makes time speed away, so that you would find yourself upon the homeward voyage hardly realising that several months have been spent on the coast, were it not that an inspection of your clothes shows that the climate has made ravages upon them, and that after quietly looking yourself over you find that your face is pale and drawn, and that you have lost much of the energy with which you started.

There can be no doubt that the climate of West Africa is most unkind! Seemingly pleasant and outwardly propitious, so that new arrivals, with a courage based on ignorance, deride the cautious habits of those who know, it nevertheless wages an insidious combat against health, and more often than not succeeds. But there is a fascination about the country which leads you to discount this and other ills, and draws you back to it, even although you might be living comfortably in more agreeable surroundings. It is strange, too, how always when the climate seizes its victim, the climate is the last to be blamed. You hear it said, "poor So-and-So has gone at last! Strange! for he was an old coaster, and I can't understand *his* dying!" Then the whole matter is discussed, and it is almost invariably the case that some cause other than the climate is found to account for death. The man's constitution was such that the doctors in England ought not to have passed him as fitted to live in West Africa, or he has been playing golf or tennis and caught a chill. "So foolish of him! for he must have known what a chill would mean to him!" In fact, it is demonstrated with sufficient satisfaction that the climate is blameless, and that the whole responsibility rests with the individual.

At Accra, which is the seat of Government, and where the majority of the Europeans live, the temperature is by no means unpleasant. There is nearly always a mild breeze blowing inland from the sea, which renders the use of punkahs unnecessary. A blanket is often needed at night, and

always a warm wrap for the afternoon drive. The use of the word drive may be perhaps misleading, because horses and carriages are somewhat of a luxury. The famous go-cart is the vehicle generally used. This very uncomfortable mode of conveyance is calculated to tire the most robust after an hour's experience. It is a cart on two wheels, on springs that have no spring in them ; it has a long pole in front with a crossbar at the end of it, and it is drawn by Kroo boys. The pole-boy has to have a certain amount of training to keep the pole at the right angle, or else the cart tips backwards, and you find yourself in a very undignified and unenviable position! There are as a rule three boys—two behind the cart pushing, and the pole-boy. They go along at a fair rate, and on the whole it seems rather marvellous that they manage it as well as they do, for it is an awkward, clumsy contrivance.

I remember once very nearly having a nasty accident when driving in a go-cart with my husband. We had been out along one of the roads somewhat further than usual, and it was dark when we reached the compound of Government House. Suddenly, without a word of warning, down went the pole, and we were precipitated forward at the risk of breaking our noses on the ground in front of us, the pole-boy darting forward with the cry, "master, something bite me!" After we had recovered from this hurried exit, the go-cart lantern was obtained—for every go-cart has a lantern attached to it—for the purpose of examining the bite. We found the Kroo boy nursing his left foot, and there, sure enough, at the back of the heel was a small puncture from which blood was oozing. It was evidently a scorpion sting. Immediately there was a hue-and-cry for the scorpion. The most careful search was made without success, but at last, just as the search was being abandoned, he was discovered close to the injured Kroo boy, who, in fact, was nearly sitting upon him! He was a large black one, with tail erect ready to make another attack. As soon as he was discovered the scorpion made a dart for the Kroo boys who held the lantern, and it was the funniest sight, for they all stampeded as if pursued by some ferocious animal. The poor scorpion was arrested in his onslaught by a blow from my husband's stick, which knocked off his two lobster-like claws and disposed of him. In the meantime the Kroo boy who had been stung was moaning piteously, but with a stiff glass of grog, which is the best internal remedy for a scorpion or centipede sting, he soon recovered equanimity enough to hobble off to the Kroo boys' hut, there to have his wound attended to and dressed.

The Kroo boys used to be a much better set a few years back than they are now; the independence of the age appears to have attacked them, so that they are beginning to fancy themselves overmuch. They are imported for labour all along the coast, as the native often considers himself too superior a person for any servile work. My experience of the Kroo boy is a domestic one, and I have always found him willing, honest, and eager to do his best; but I cannot say that he is clean, for *bouquet d'Afrique* is one of his possessions which it seems impossible for him to part with! We used Kroo boys about the house to carry water, scrub floors, etc. Their great idea is to buy as many things as possible and pack them away in wooden boxes for their return home, to show their friends what wealth they have accumulated.

The landing of a party of Kroo boys at their native town on the Kroo coast is one of the quaintest sights imaginable. Long before the steamer nears the town a babel of voices and general bustle begins. Boxes, powder kegs, and guns are brought out, and all the worldly wealth of the party is disposed along the deck of the steamer ready to be slung over the side when the canoes arrive. The steamer nears the shore; already it has been descried from the beach, from which may be seen several canoes dashing out to pick up the party, and more especially the goods which it is bringing with it, for I fancy that these are regarded as of far more importance than the owners, who are generally treated with but scant ceremony. The canoes near the steamer, and then commences a noise which baffles description. The canoe-men shout their terms for passages, friends are recognised, and called to from stentorian throats in language guttural and without modulation. Finally, the canoes come alongside, and then the fun for the onlooker commences.

Fierce gesticulations take the place of friendly greetings: boxes and kegs are slung over the side and snatched at, the rope securing them being pulled here and there by competitors for the traffic. The Kroo boys on the steamer all simultaneously shout their directions as to the canoe in which their respective belongings are to be embarked, and pandemonium rages. More than one canoe is upset in the struggle, and drifts to leeward with the occupants bobbing up and down in the water rescuing boxes, but never leaving the canoe, which, righted and baled out, soon receives it freight and returns to the scene of action. At last the captain of the steamer notifies that he can give no further time; the last boxes are slung over, and a few turns of the screw are given as a warning to the Kroo boys to hasten their departure. Even then the warning is unheeded by many, and it is only when the steamer begins to move ahead that the end is reached. The remaining Kroo boys one after the other jump into the sea, disappear for a few seconds under water, and are soon seen swimming for the canoes. The noise of departure grows less and less as the steamer gains way, the canoes race for the beach, and once more peace prevails.

The Kroo boys are expert boatmen and fishermen, and appear to be as much at home in the water as on land. They make excellent seamen, and every British cruiser or gunboat on the West Coast of Africa has its complement of Kroo boys dressed as British bluejackets. Very proud are they of their uniform, and of the service in which they are enrolled.

When at home, fishing is their staple employment. I remember once on an outward voyage, the steamer

Life in West Africa

in which I was travelling stopped to land a small consignment of cargo in the midst of a fleet of canoes, all the occupants of which were fishing. In one close to the steamer was a brawny angler with three lines—one on each of his big toes, one in his right hand, while with his left hand he baled out the water from his leaking canoe with a sort of wooden shovel. It was Sunday morning, and my husband was leaning over the side of the steamer watching the man. Suddenly he looked up and said, "morning, master." Asked if he could speak English, he replied, "small, small," which means a little, probably a very little. Then ensued a conversation in pidgin-English about fishing and the size of the fish caught, the man complaining that he could that morning get no sport. My husband said at last to him, "ah, you see, to-day is Sunday, and the fish will not bite." Straight from the canoe came the ready answer, "master, fish no sabbe (Anglice—do not know) Sunday." The man had served on board a British cruiser, and knew the difference between Sunday and other days. The answer was a clever one, and worthy of a higher state of civilisation.

Kroo boys have the funniest ideas in making purchases for their home-going. On one occasion

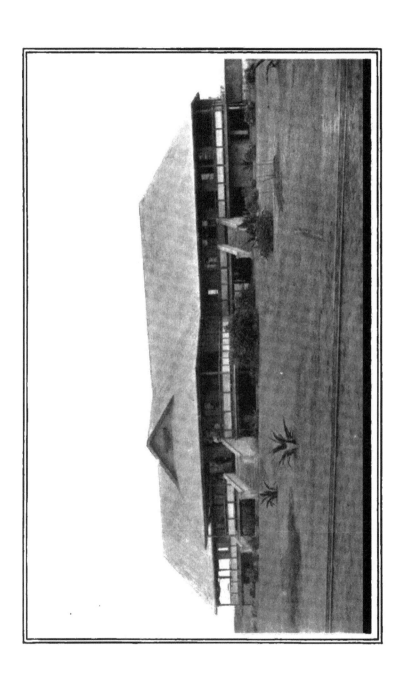

Life in West Africa

about twenty of them bought brass instruments, and formed themselves into a band. The noises and squeals that were produced were rather dreadful, and we got the full benefit of them, for our "boys" were the moving spirits, and arranged the band practices to be held in our compound, until a stop was put to it.

Sunday morning is a great day for the Kroo boys. Their delight is to dress up in fine clothes and parade the streets, first, if they are on good terms with their master or mistress, showing themselves for approval and admiration in their grand costumes. One perhaps will be dressed in some sort of uniform; another in a frock coat, brown boots, and a tall white hat; a third in a cricket blazer, white flannel trousers, and patent leather boots. They then go forth, followed by an admiring crowd, to swagger before their less fortunate friends. On these occasions the photographer is generally not without a visit from them, for they love to stand posed before him in all their finery, and in attitudes the clumsiest and stiffest. Their outing ends with an enormous meal at about twelve o'clock, after which they sleep until it is time for them to get the go-cart ready for church or the drive.

CHAPTER XXIII

SERVANTS AND NATIVE LETTERS

WHEN one goes for the first time to West Africa, and realises that there are no women servants, and that all the household work is in the hands of men, or "boys," as they are called, one naturally imagines all sorts of disadvantages, and that it will never be possible to get along at all. But I never found it so in practice. The boys are very respectful and anxious to learn, and I was soon accustomed to having them about me. They are as handy as women servants, and are to be trusted in looking after your clothes and keeping everything in order. They are very faithful and, I am sure, serve you to the best of their ability; often, however, they fail you at a critical moment, not because they mean to do so, but because anything out of the ordinary run upsets them, and they lose their heads. Another great disadvantage to them is that most of them do not understand English, and often pretend to have understood what you have said, and go straightway and do the very reverse!

As a rule, your house-servants are natives : they are always known as " boys," never as servants, but we had a Kroo boy who was with us for eight years, and worked his way up to head house boy. He was a very superior young fellow, being the son of one of the chiefs of a town on the Kroo coast. He and I were the greatest friends, and I am sure he would have done anything for me, except give up getting into debt. This was a very favourite pastime with him, and when he was in great straits he would come and throw himself upon my mercy to help him from being arrested by his creditors. He used always to be very busy in my bedroom whenever he had anything of a disagreeable nature to unfold, and would begin a long story of how badly he had been treated. So-and-So had borrowed money from him, and now that he required it to pay a bill he could not get it. After sifting his long story you would find that he had himself borrowed the money instead of having lent it, and that he was now being pressed for it.

How servants fail at critical moments may be illustrated by a very amusing incident which happened to us last Christmas Day (1899). We had a large dinner-party. Everything had gone splendidly, and the roast beef of old England was not wanting, for this had been sent out in ice as a Christmas box from our good friend Mr. A. L. Jones, of Liverpool. The time for bringing in the tinned plum puddings was at hand ; they were to be brought in decorated, in order to keep up the idea of home, with a tropical sprig not unlike holly. A pause began, it grew worse and worse, crackers were pulled, and conversation was kept floating, still the puddings did not arrive! I began to feel uneasy, and my eyes wandered down the table to see if the Private Secretary had realised that there was something wrong. None of the servants were in the room except the head butler, a man we had had only a few weeks, who was proving but a bad bargain. He stood immovable; all my nods and winks at him were without avail. I began to think something serious had overtaken the puddings, and so it had! for the cook who had to pour the brandy over them, which it was arranged should be given him by the butler, had been assaulted by him. I saw the Private Secretary slip out of the room, and knew that something unusual must have happened. To make a long story short, the butler had mislaid his keys, and, when the brandy was required, they were not forthcoming. The cook was a very intelligent, methodical man, and this pause and wait were very annoying to him, so that, when the keys were at last found and the brandy given out, he made some remark about the other man's slowness. The butler seized the brandy bottle and swung it round, bringing it with great force down upon the cook's face. After doing this he ran into the dining-room, and took up his position behind the Governor, avoiding my glances when I wanted to attract his notice. Needless to say, he never again had the opportunity of standing behind the Governor's chair. This is a fair sample of annoying incidents that may take place in your household; but one's guests are always very good-natured and say, "it is only Africa!"

Christmas besides being the hottest season is generally also the gayest. The races take place at Accra towards the end of December, and are the great event of the year. The natives show very keen interest in them, and the course is a mass of bright and gorgeous colour. The youngsters climb the trees so as to get a good view of the proceedings, and all have made up their minds to enjoy themselves, and try their best to succeed.

Servants and Native Letters

Horses are sometimes sent from Lagos, and this adds to the excitement of the meeting, and is apt to upset the racing men when the Governor's Cup is carried away to another colony.

The racecourse is by no means a bad one, and a substantial grand-stand, built of stone and concrete, has been erected by Government. It lies about midway between the towns of Accra and Christianborg, in the neighbourhood of the bungalows built for the Government officers who have to reside at headquarters, and is fairly level throughout. For days before the races take place the course is thoroughly overhauled: the grass is cut, posts are renewed, and the course roped in. Elaborate race-cards are printed, and admission to the grand-stand is fixed. The arrangements are all carefully thought out, and made by a committee of management, and the money prizes are usually worth winning. There is much fun over the training of the horses and their trials, and every evening there is a crowd on the course to see them galloping. There is very little betting on the races, owing to the introduction of the French pari-mutuel system, which is much resorted to and creates a fund of interest. Horses suffer a great deal from the climate, and require constant care and

attention. A man who owns a horse and can keep it in fair health is looked upon by his brother officers as a hero of no small degree.

The School Exhibition and Sale of Work, held in the Government schoolroom, also takes place at the end of the year. All schools throughout the Colony can compete, and it is really a most interesting affair. Prizes and awards are given by Government, and the exhibition is opened by the Governor. The band of the Hausa force is in attendance, there is a guard of honour for His Excellency, and everything possible is done to make the exhibition and sale successful. The competition is very keen, so that it is sometimes difficult to select your purchases where all are so good. The Roman Catholic Mission Schools generally manage to take the first prizes for needlework, and the Basel Mission Schools for carpentry, etc.

The native lads—I refer more especially to those in the coast towns, who have come into contact with Europeans—are very anxious to learn, and become regular attendants at the schools, of which there are very many in the Colony. In fact, they are absolutely voracious in their acquisition of knowledge. Many begin rather late, and it is amusing to see big lads of fifteen learning their A B C in the infant classes. Until recently there have been very few books excepting the Bible readily accessible to native youths, and that, I think, is why their letters, for they never lose an opportunity for putting pen to paper, are couched in such quaint and, at times, old-fashioned language.

The following are specimens of letters written by the average native. The first is from a lad who was at the time a messenger in one of the Government offices, and is an application to the Governor for a better and more lucrative appointment. His appeal on the ground that he has not enough work to do, or as he puts it, " My position will not let me improving at whatever when I come to office. I sitting down like wood doing nothing till the office close," is excellent, and so also is his apology for his handwriting. The second is an application from an old friend of my husband for cartridges for his Swinburne rifle, or, as he calls it, "Swimbung Riffle." Can anything equal the expression in this letter—" I am burning down always like a candle while my position requires my burning like a lamp filled with oil"? The applicant had his cartridges. He is one of the best natives I know, and prosperous, but whether the cartridges were expended against the elephants at a place called N'Kaneku, and brought his affairs "to a better change," I cannot say. The third is from my cook, who writes from Accra, giving the news of the town, and asking that some money may be sent to him to keep him going until our return. Quarshie and Joseph who are referred to in the letter were two of his fellow-servants. The expression "I have put my mind on you as narrated me before you went" means "I remember what you said to me before you left," and "therefore I cannot step my foot to anywhere" means "I do not intend to get other employment." "Three man-of-war landed at Accra" is rather a startling announcement, but evidently their arrival off Accra is what is meant.

"USSHER TOWN, ACCRA,

"31st January, 1891.

"SIR,—I beg that you will be so good enough to strive manly to get me another employment for substituting of my present position. Dont be considered that my handwriting of which I having it now is very bad, but I know many a man whose hand using like my yet they were employed, but I mean not say that I was not employed at all,

S 333

I mean my position will not let me improving at whatever when I come to office I sitting down like wood doing nothing till the office close. And if there is a knif it will not be taking to cut any thing it gets to damage. I learn experience that every man wishes to receive eyes open etc. and I wish too to. get my eyes open, so I therefore lay hold of you with my supernatural power like Jacob the father of Israelities when he laid hold of the angel, said he except thou wilt bless me before I let you, and may I trouble you the same manner to help me to obtain some place, many my friends and relations they learn to work for their prosper and progress but I was very much sorry for mine. Please let my supplication undergoing straight to success with good result after the peruse of this note and I should think you will never delay or put aside to let go for the chief's deeply consideration to transfire me for some station, I shall feel obliged if you kindly to let me have good reply as early date.

> " I am your obedient servant
>
> "(sgd.)   J. ——."

> "TEPONG, 24*th March*.

"SIR,—I have been trying from year to years thinking of what way I could make my fortune, but no success in what way or other. I am burning down always like a candle, while my position requires my burning like a lamp filled with oil. To be a trader like other friends would cost my ruin. I get large farm of palms but no means or men to work it. Being afraid to loss the surplus of the little means I saved from Government, I bought a gun with it, and have made up my mind to send an expedition against the elephants at a placed called N'Kaneku, to see whether this will bring my affairs to a better change. Being as a single gun is not sufficient for this Work, and that you have presented me with Swimbung Riffle now lying down in my possession without any use by want of cathridges. The confidence I have and the fillial fear I get towards you encourage me to send this bearer to you begging your Honour to take upon yourself to persuade His Excellency the Governor to allow the Commander of the Forces to send me 100 rounds cathridges of the Swimbung Riffle for the business I am undertaking. I hope this may meet your Honour in a good health.

> "I am, sir,
>> "Your obedient servant,
>>> "_____."

The cook's amusing letter is a happy blend of general news and business :—

Servants and Native Letters

"GARDEN STREET,
　　"JAMES TOWN, ACCRA,
　　　"28.9.1900.

"DEAR SIR,—I should think that you have reached safely. Inform Miss that I convey my best compliments to her, and I presume that Miss have met her daughter in a good health. More also I beg to announce that Quarshie convey his compliments to both of you. I have put my mind on you as narrated me before you went therefore I cannot step my foot to anywhere. At present I beg to designate that I am not doing a work at anywhere which therefore hope you may despatch me some money to look after myself as you aforesaid. Joseph was engaged by Mr. —— as a Chief Steward. No intelligence to be narrated but Mr. —— his going to inspection during this ultimo. From since you went there is no dinner party to be called, therefore all the white men remind you as usual. On the 27th day of September three man of war landed at Accra and the soldiers therein came to Accra including with Volunters police and soldiers were gone to palade ground. With band and everything but I dont know the reason which call their attention to be made that and I should think if you were in town of Accra they will done more than what took place. On the receipt of this kindly inform me how my leaving will because you have conveyed me a word

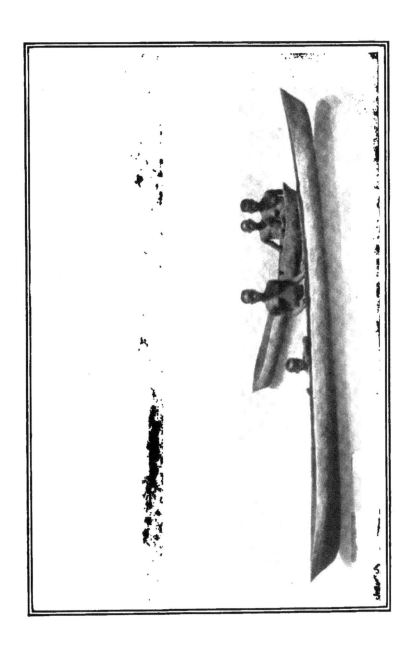

not to stept to anywhere, therefore I hope you will be no doubt to let me receive the money as you aforementioned. Inform Miss that I want to furnish her two photos be made enlargement and if she could manage to get one of Photo's men to do it then she must try and reply me, so as to dispatch it by first coming steamer. Nothing strange to be announced than my best compliments to self and all.

        " Yours respectfully,

"(sgd.)   ——, Cook."

CHAPTER XXIV

ADVANCEMENT OF THE NATIVES

FOR many years past the Basel Missionary Society had done excellent work by teaching handicrafts — carpentering, cabinet - making, and forge-work, and it has met with considerable success. The Gold Coast natives are celebrated up and down the coast as good carpenters, and readily find work if they care to leave their country in search of it, and in all the villages at the back of Accra and elsewhere there is always to be found a forge and carpenter's bench. At the former, hinges, bolts, and even very creditable locks and keys are turned out, and at the latter doors and window-frames.

The Government has recently started a technical school at Accra, where the theory of carpentering is taught, and where the lads under instruction acquire a practical knowledge in more finished work, such as panelling, grooving, and the like. The Public Works Department apprentice masons, and perhaps the best instruction which has been

Advancement of the Natives

given to the natives was the building of a very fine church at Accra. The stone used for this church was quarried by convict labour. It is hard, red-coloured stone, and most effective for church architecture. The masons were taught to square and prepare it, and the effect of the instruction is apparent from the improvement which has since taken place in the erection of the dwelling-houses of the natives, many of them being built of squared stones with rounded archways as entrances, similar in character to the Norman archways used in the church. Unfortunately the native seldom sits down and counts the cost of the proposed house. His mind booms big at the idea of being a house-owner, and he determines upon a massive stone structure, with stone pillars supporting a veranda, and all the latest improvements. The work is commenced with much dash and energy, and all goes well for a time. Then, before the house is half completed, the money begins to give out, the number of workmen employed has to be curtailed, and the end crowns his labour after only many years of saving. As a consequence, the native towns in West Africa have a dilapidated appearance because there are so many unfinished houses.

Advancement of the Natives

The fashion of the educated native to clothe himself in European dress has brought tailoring and boot-making to the front, and in Accra, Cape Coast, and elsewhere there is quite a brisk trade in clothes and boots, and a constant demand for such costumes as appeal to native taste. In the matter of dress there is quite a keen competition, especially on Sundays, when frock coats, tall hats, patent leather boots, and kid gloves are sported everywhere. Nor are the native ladies behindhand, and, but that the combination of colours is not always successful, some of them dress well, and look particularly imposing.

A wedding of educated natives is a very considerable function. Long before the important day arrives, the question of dress arises and is discussed. Very often the dresses of the bride and bridesmaids are ordered from England. Orange blossom for the bride is a necessity, and when the day arrives she stands before the altar in a white satin or silk dress generally decorated with silver leaves and orange blossom, a tulle veil, and carries a bouquet of flowers in her hands. The bridesmaids have on new frocks. All wear white kid gloves and new boots, and the men are resplendent in frock coats and tall white hats.

Advancement of the Natives

Before the wedding ceremony cards of invitation "to the nuptials" of Miss So-and-So to Mr. So-and-So are sent out, and I have been invited more than once. The following is an invitation sent to me. It was printed in gold letters on a pink card about the size of a lady's visiting-card :—

HYMENEAL.

—

Mr. Thomas ——
and
Miss ——
Will be happy of your company to the
Celebration of
Their nuptials
On Thursday, 28th December, 1892, at Trinity Chapel,
At 2 o'clock p.m., from there
To Leopold Street.

After the ceremony an adjournment is made to the house of the bride's parents, or, it may be, to the house of a friend, where refreshments are served. On these occasions the bride and bridegroom sit apart at the head of the room, and the bridesmaids and the other ladies range themselves on seats in a row along the side of it. It is rather a dismal business, I am told, for the ladies decline to move, and the men are too bashful to single one out, and to go and talk to her.

343

Advancement of the Natives

As in England, Christmas-time is the season for dances, but as European ladies are so few the evening's amusement has to be helped out by music, and when the community is very energetic theatricals are attempted. At the first start, as in every other place, no one will take part, or the part assigned to each is not the one wanted; a general squabble arises, then everyone becomes very amiable, and on the eventful night thorough enjoyment ensues for both actors and audience. The hostess on these occasions has an anxious time until it is all over, never knowing which of her theatrical company will fail at the last moment. It has happened that one of the principal characters has fainted when dressing for his part, which was then hurriedly taken by the stage-manager. It was a woman's part; the real man for it was short, the stage-manager tall, so the effect of the short skirts intended to be long ones was very comical, though no doubt it added to the relish of the scene.

Once we had some waxworks, and very successful they were, for we had an excellent showman, who in official life was the local magistrate. During the performance I turned to one of my native guests and asked him whether he had seen waxworks before. He answered, "yes, in the London streets." I could not say whether he meant a Punch and Judy show, or the wax figures in the shop windows, and I never learnt, as I feared to ask. I believe that the first theatricals ever held in the Gold Coast were some which I arranged in 1892. There were no European ladies at Accra then, except myself, so all the parts were taken by good-natured men. The ladies' parts were much run after; great raids were made upon my wardrobe, and I should have had very little left, so vain is man, had I not been quite firm as to what they might not take. The theatricals were a brilliant success. We invited all the principal native Government clerks to see them, and they went away delighted; those who had not been to England never having seen anything like it before. These theatricals took such a hold upon the native mind that some of the more enterprising formed a dramatic company, and asked one of the European officials to help them. We went to one of their performances, a very ambitious representation of scenes from *The Merchant of Venice*. The costumes were native cloths and head-dresses, much resembling the classic style of ancient days. The stage was very small and primitive, as most social things on the Gold Coast are, but the per-

formance was very creditable, and the acting of
some was really good.

A few years back a grand ball was given by the
natives, in honour of the Governor and myself.
We arrived with our suite, and opened the ball;
I had politely to reject many offers of partners, one
man persisting that he was a steward, and therefore
had a right to dance with me. Supper came along
at the proper time, and I was taken in by the
District Commissioner of Accra, whose services
had been enlisted to assist in making the ball a
success. On my other side sat the president of
the evening, a native gentleman. Among the
features of the supper were hot potatoes, which
played a very important part all through, but the
greatest when I nearly had them all poured down
my back. My supporters in some way passed the
dish over my head, and then took the opportunity
of discussing who was to propose the Governor's
health. I cleverly evaded sundry knocks on my
head, and suggested that the dish would be safer
on the table! The hint was taken and the dish
released, but the "health" question had not yet
been decided. Then began a series of whispers and
coat-tail pulling behind my back; neither would
give way as to whose duty it was to make the

GIRLS AT A WATER-HOLE

Face page 346

Advancement of the Natives

speech, and when at last the time came, both started to their feet together. Everyone was by then in roars of laughter; they both sat down again, and at last the health was proposed by the gentleman on my left, and drunk so enthusiastically by him that when he returned to the ballroom he found a comfortable seat on the floor. No ladies, I being the only white woman, were admitted to the supper-room. They sat in a room which could be seen from where we were, and seemed to be having a very silent and solemn meal. West African ladies do not take a very prominent part in social life, as they have not thrown off to any great extent the ancient ways when women were always considered inferior beings by the superior man. I have met some charming African ladies, and am glad to say that in my ten years' experience of the Gold Coast each year improved the position of women, and to-day they—I am speaking of educated women—are not the slaves to their husbands that they were a few years ago. It has been most interesting to watch the growth and civilisation of the community, and it really seems marvellous how Accra has advanced within the last few years, even in the matter of entertainments.

Just after my arrival last November a ball was

very kindly given by the native ladies and gentlemen to welcome me back. It was done entirely by themselves. All Europeans were invited to it, and everything went well. The rooms were prettily decorated, and there were programmes for dancing. Ladies and gentlemen sat together for supper, and the champagne and turkeys were not handed out of the windows to expectant friends as on previous occasions, but, alas! potatoes were still a feature of the supper! I really enjoyed the ball, and received a message from the King of Accra after supper to honour him with a dance. I sent back what I thought was a diplomatic answer, to the effect that English ladies did not care about dancing after supper. The old man thereupon settled himself down to a game of chess, which was much more suited to him than dancing with me. He was very proud to tell me that he had learnt the game from an English lady.

Old King Tackie and I were great friends, and he always declared that he made fetish over the surf whenever I was landing or embarking, so as to ensure my safety. Those who have not been through the surf cannot imagine it. Sometimes it is no worse than a roughish English beach, but when it is bad it takes all your courage to go through. The boat climbs up to the top of the wave and then rushes down the other side, while the foam breaks below. When you are down one wave there is another confronting you which has to be climbed. The boatmen manage the boats splendidly, singing all the time, which does not help your nerves, however much it may help them to push along. Although going through the surf is attended with great danger, accidents are very few and far between. Your first question, on being met on the steamer at Accra, is, what is the surf like? When assured that it is not at all bad, this means that it is not good, and you know what you will have to face.

CHAPTER XXV

EFFECTS OF BRITISH RULE

UNTIL the last few years Europeans at Head
Quarters lived generally in the native towns
of Accra and Christianborg, but, thanks to the
initiative and insistence of my husband, all this
has now been changed. Bungalows, raised some
ten feet from the ground on iron pillars, have been
built on sanitary sites away from these towns, much
to the promotion of health and comfort. It must
have been terrible formerly when the bungalows
did not exist. Many a man's heart must have
sunk on his arrival at finding himself in the rooms
allotted to him; for on leaving England he had
doubtless pictured the furnished quarters attached
to his appointment as a small palace. Sometimes the wife also arrived to inhabit those "furnished quarters," and there is a story told of a
bride, a short time after her arrival, sitting on a
rickety table, crying bitterly, and asking where
the furniture was. But all this is changed now,

and the bungalows are really pretty little houses with nice pieces of ground round them.

Some have turned this ground to account, and tried to make a garden : others content themselves by keeping the place free from weeds. I say "tried" to make a garden, for it is a somewhat hopeless task, as water is so scarce, and the soil is very sandy, dry, and unfertile. The long dry season is a terrible enemy to flower and vegetable growth, which seems quite hopeless then. Nothing foreign to the country thrives really well, even in the wet season, except zinnias, gelardias, and sun-flowers, and flowers are quite a luxury in Accra, even at the best of times. I was very fond of my garden, and tried various seeds, but all without much success. The sea-air stunts the growth of shrubs, and most days there is so strong a sea-breeze blowing that it bends trees and shrubs all in one direction permanently.

We had two tennis-grounds at Government House, and a croquet-ground; one cannot call them lawns, for they are made out of "swish," a mixture of water and a special kind of earth which is dried by the sun. The grounds play well, and are as fast for tennis as an asphalt court. It was always a great pleasure to me on my reception days to see all three grounds used at once. It so happens in that horrible climate that, although tennis-players are plentiful, there are not even four men who feel able to undertake the exertion of a game of tennis, and yet these young fellows only a few months back had perhaps been some of England's most energetic players.

The club is one of Accra's attractions. It is prettily and comfortably fitted, and the men meet there in the afternoons to discuss the topics of the day, and—shall I say it?—sometimes to squabble; but differences do not last for ever and a day, and into small communities squabbles must enter, to vary the monotony of existence. Ladies are admitted to the club; all the English papers are provided, and on a mail-day the scene is very animated.

Close to the club-house are the golf links and polo ground. The golf links are small, only five holes, but they are by no means bad, and my husband has had many a good game upon them. The golf links and cricket ground, for there is a very good cricket club, were kept in order by a gang of prisoners specially told off for the purpose.

The gaol at Accra for long-sentence prisoners is in the old English fort, known as James' Fort.

Effects of British Rule

It is not very satisfactory for prison purposes, as the prisoners have to be kept associated in large wards holding from ten to twenty men each ; but considering this great drawback, and the difficulty of finding suitable native warders, the discipline maintained is on the whole very satisfactory. I have more than once been over the prison, and have been struck by the neatness and order that prevail. Much has been done in recent years to take advantage of the prisoner's detention to teach him a handicraft. Both at Accra, and at Elmina, where there is a penal establishment for the western province of the Colony, there are classes for boot-making, tailoring, carpentering, mat-making, and weaving. Thus the prison is alive with labour, and very neat work is turned out. The prisoners' canvas suits are made up in the tailors' class, where also all the uniforms worn by the native warders and other Government officials (sanitary inspectors, hospital attendants, court bailiffs, and so forth) are made up. All prisoners' sleeping-mats are made in the two prisons, from rushes gathered by the prisoners themselves. Very creditable cupboards, boxes, and bird-cages are manufactured, and excellent boots are turned out.

Effects of British Rule

The prisoners also prepare and cook their own food, so that the prison is, in fact, not only a penal, but an industrial establishment, doing excellent work, and teaching each man a handicraft which may furnish him with occupation on his release, and perhaps, by giving him an occupation, deter him from the further commission of crime.

The "mark" system is also in force, by which convicts can, by good conduct while in gaol, obtain the remission of portions of their sentences. This system is working admirably, and assists materially in the maintenance of discipline. Men of good conduct after a certain time receive good-conduct stripes, and with them certain small privileges.

Once, when out for my evening drive, I met a gang of prisoners who had been sent out across the lagoon to gather rushes for mat-making. They were marching quietly along, but without a warder. My husband who was with me was thunderstruck, and halted the gang, asking if any one of them could speak English: a man with good-conduct stripes on his arm stepped out and said he could. Being asked where the warder in charge was, the convict replied that he was coming on behind with another gang. "But who is in charge of this gang?" was the next question. "I am," said the man. "You see, sir," he continued in very good English, "I am a good-conduct man, and I am not likely to let any of the prisoners run away." He evidently no longer regarded himself in the same category as the others whom he designated as prisoners, while he was the good-conduct man. The gang returned safely to the prison, but I am inclined to think that the arrangement under which the warder thought himself justified in relinquishing the control over a portion of his gang was not continued.

An amusing story was told me of a convict, a man sentenced at first to death. His sentence had been commuted to penal servitude for life, and this change in the man's position was duly communicated to him. Like all African natives he manifested no surprise, but asked whether he would be permitted to join the other prisoners, and have the same food and work as they had. Being answered in the affirmative, he replied, "very well, master, then I will stay," being evidently under the impression that it was quite a matter for his decision, and that, by deciding to live on in prison, he was conferring a great favour !

The hospital is another important institution in Accra which deserves special mention. Of recent years it has been greatly improved and enlarged, and the employment by the Government of trained English nurses has done much to alleviate suffering and save life. These ladies are most energetic and devoted to their work, faithfully nursing and caring for the European patients who are their first charge, while not neglecting to give attention to cases in the native wards. It is difficult to realise how the Gold Coast did so long without their valuable assistance. A pretty little bungalow has been built in the hospital grounds to accommodate two nursing sisters, who take a pride in their garden and quarters, and lead a very happy as well as a very useful life. Attached to the hospital is a fine and well-fitted laboratory, which is doing good work in connection with the study of malarious mosquitoes and other horrors.

The Botanical Station is twenty-six miles away from Accra, on a range of hills some fourteen hundred feet high, at Aburi, which is a lovely spot. There roses, geraniums, and many of our best-known English flowers grow in profusion, but the station is of course given up to the growth of plants of an economic value, and it has been the means of considerably increasing the cultivation of cocoa, rubber, and other products, besides

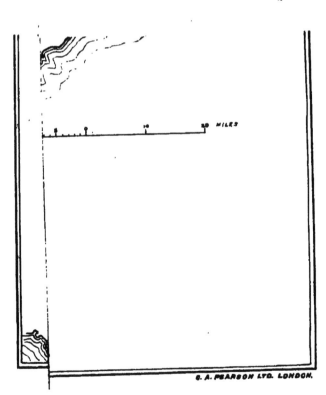

MILES

C. A. PEARSON LTD. LONDON.

stimulating the natives to greater efforts in agriculture. In the midst of the garden, and commanding magnificent views of the surrounding scenery, is the Government Sanatorium, a well-built and comfortable house for the use of invalids, and those who require a few days' recruiting after the heavy steamy air of the coast, or after a severe attack of fever.

INDEX

Index

Index

Index

Index

Index

PLYMOUTH: W. BRENDON AND SON, PRINTERS.

Ingram Content Group UK Ltd.
Milton Keynes UK
UKHW020916140323
418553UK00007B/578